The events   alled
from the best of my memory and/or old journals I had kept, who
read it, may not like everything they read, but unfortunately sometimes
the truth is the hardest thing to hear. All of the dialogue has been
reconstructed from memory; it may not be word for word, but the nature
of what was said is accurate. It was suggested by some of my closest
friends and family that I take my unbelievable story and life lessons
learned with Sara and not only write them down, but publish a book for
others to read and try to grasp the hell I lived. I know I'm not alone in
what I had gone through and there are other people out there who are
living a similar life that I lived. I thought that if I wrote this book, sharing
the struggles I faced being married to someone who was mentally,
emotionally and sometimes physically abusive (not to mention
controlling, completely unpredictable and manipulative), there may be
some small chance that one of these people living in a similar hell may
read it and find that there is a way out. There is hope for a better life.

I will say, writing these memories, (or in most cases nightmares)
down was very therapeutic but not often easy. I do not regret anything I
wrote in this book. I wanted everything to be honest, factual, uncensored
and descriptive, and I believe in order to do it right, it couldn't have been
done any other way. Some of the chapters were next to impossible to
write because of the nature of the situations I found myself in, and how
personal the memories were, and I hesitated including them in this book,
however I felt it was needed to show the lengths Sara would go to to
manipulate, degrade and brainwash me, ultimately leading to the
destruction of our marriage.

It took me a very long time to recognize and admit I was a victim of
abuse, especially from a woman. Being a man's man, that wasn't easy.
After my admission, I had to take a look back at the big picture and
realize my intentions were always good, but I was just manipulated,
brainwashed and beaten down to the point of alienating virtually
everyone away from me. I was lost and spiraling quickly down a very
dark, destructive path. I am still working on standing tall and holding my
head up after many years of abuse. I am not ashamed of myself any
longer, and have become comfortable speaking out on this subject. I am
a much different man today than I was back then. This is my story. This
was the life I lived for 12 years, the life that still haunts me; even today.

What a Shame, what a shame
To judge a life that you can't change
What a shame to have to beg you to
See we're not all the same
What a shame

-Shinedown

Preface

I grew up in small town Minnesota and was always somewhat of a quiet, or most often a shy child. My parents raised me to be respectful to everyone, to always give and to help others in need, which I made habit of in my adult life. I never got into fights, yet was bullied nearly every day as an adolescent, but attempted to avoid conflict at all costs. I took Martial Arts for many years as an adolescent which taught me patience, mental and physical endurance, self-control and self-respect. I made it just shy of being awarded the black belt before I quit to join the High School Drumline. I smiled a lot, enjoyed life, and held a tremendous amount of innocence and purity in my upbringing. My dad raced stock cars for many years and I learned quickly how to work a wrench and be creative in fixing things. I didn't make friends easily, but the friends I did make, I held with very high regard. I was loyal, honest and overall a good human being. I had always been shy around girls and was frequently oblivious to any interest they may have found in me. I only had two girlfriends, by some miracle, throughout my entire life before I was in high school. All of this, which made me who I was, changed once I became involved with Sara.

When I got up enough guts to ask my friend, Sara, to try dating at 17 years old, I had no idea what I was getting in to. With young love, it didn't matter what negative situations developed, I either didn't see it, or ignored it because I finally had a girlfriend. She was more popular than I was; I had never been even remotely popular and when I became involved with Sara, people finally noticed me. I was accepted, or so it seemed. I figured I could soften her abrasive edges a little and we could make this relationship work. It was August 17th, 1998, and we were now officially dating. In the beginning, I do remember having a lot of good times with her. Things weren't always bad. We were more than friends, but still had that element of good friends, so things were easy. I didn't feel like I had to be anyone other than who I was, and I didn't expect her to be anyone different than who she was. We would do everything together, and we would do nothing together and enjoy every minute of it. It was always exciting because we each had our best friend there by our side to take things to the next step in a relationship, such as kissing, holding hands, and then the other things that go along with being in a romantic relationship; we'd experience these things together.

My point? We were like any other teenage romance. It was not uncommon for us to do sweet gestures for each other like writing little notes in our lockers at school to each other, or meeting each other for lunch. I'm sure we made some people sick. Then things began to slowly change. As time went on, and we spent virtually every waking moment together, I began to feel the suffocation of a poisonous relationship creeping in, but by the time I realized this, I was too deep into it and didn't know what to do; the brainwashing had begun. Admittedly, there was a fairly significant amount of fear I developed towards Sara. Along the way, I had friends I turned to here and there, but eventually, telling people some of the things that were going on was far too embarrassing to share. I kept things to myself and tried to work through them alone, or just simply ignore them. I reverted to music quite a bit over the 12 years I spent with Sara. It seems like there was always a band or a song that spoke so clearly to me and would somehow advise me of what I could do, if anything, or simply give me that feeling that there is hope; there is someone who understood. *Shinedown* seemed to be my go-to band the majority of the time. Sometimes, I found a song, and listened to it over and over, feeling as if the song was written specifically for me. Even to this day, I can tell you when I hear a particular song on the radio, exactly what was going on when I heard it for the first time. Unfortunately, some songs I absolutely loved back then, I cannot listen to anymore without feeling the heartache I once felt being involved with her. Some songs, I still listen to, if only to remind me what I survived. I am where I am today because of someone who truly saved my life back on that November day. Looking back and processing everything, I can honestly say, I have no idea how I survived Sara.

This book is dedicated to those of you who are living in your own personal hell with an abusive, narcissistic, manipulating, controlling and vindictive person. When you feel like there's no way out and giving up is the only option you have, don't. There is *always* a way out, I promise.

All names have been changed to protect the identity of my children, myself and all others who have been a part of my story in one way or another.

SURVIVING SARA

The Beginning

As I began to write this chapter, I was thinking about when Sara and I got married and all the struggles we faced and the abuse that became the norm. I quickly realized that there were a plethora of memories that kept surfacing that predated our marriage. It wouldn't make much sense for me to start when we got married. I would need to dig deeper and recall the memories of life with Sara back when we began dating. I decided to call this chapter, "The Beginning", because it seemed appropriate to start there.

I remember times where I would spend virtually every waking moment with her. Whether it was at school, outside of school during drumline or evenings just hanging out, things began to fall into this rut where I noticed I was losing friends because I spent so much time with her, and who I was as an individual was slipping. I was Sara's boyfriend; period. Never mind that I was in drumline with her where I was the section leader and line captain, or that I had my own hobbies such as racing go-karts, and drumming in a band that I wanted to partake in; none of that mattered. I was to be her beckon call boy, and it wasn't long before I realized all the things I used to do often became few and far between, if at all, and I couldn't say anything about it. More often than not, when we were in drumline, we would be working in individual sections, and for one reason or another, she would leave her bass line to approach me in my snare line. She would walk in, and interrupt what we were doing to chew my ass for something that she felt was bothering her. Anything from the way I started the music, to leaving early from her house the night before. It seemed like she'd try to find something to put me on the spot and embarrass me with. She'd just glare at me with her hands on her hips, pointing her finger at me as her words just flowed. Eventually her behavior like this led to my leadership being questioned by my peers.

Back then, I was a very passive and quiet person, and never once, well rarely, responded to her insults or demands. I would just take it. It truly was embarrassing; but quite honestly, I didn't know how to argue anything. I hated confrontation and arguing. I would always lose an argument against her, or it would escalate to the point of loud yelling with others staring at us, so it was far less embarrassing to just take her shit. Even when we would meet with the whole 40 member drumline, I would try to coordinate moves or starting points and give instruction to the group and she would refuse to listen to me. I remember a common situation was when we were in the gym running our drill. "Drill" was when we'd have certain places on the gym floor we'd have to be during certain counts. Somewhat like the Superbowl halftime show with the bands, only in a gym. We'd have 8 counts to get here, or 16 counts to get back over there.

I remember very vividly one time where we were in concert formation, which is my line-the snare drums, in the middle, Sara's bass line to my left and the tenor line to my right. I began to tap off to begin the song and none of the basses played. I stopped everyone and tapped it off again; same thing. I looked over at Sara, who was just standing there, chatting with two of her other line members. She was flailing her arms, laughing and completely ignoring the fact that we were trying to rehearse. I was getting frustrated because she liked to do this especially when the instructor wasn't around. My frustration got the best of me, and I asked, "Is there a problem?" She looked right at me and said, "You mean, *besides* you?" The line began to laugh. We had a long standing rule that if you made a mistake while playing, or if you were not contributing, you got 20 push-ups. I asked her to contribute and tapped it off for a third time. Same thing, but now, her entire line was staring at me laughing. A wave of heat came over me. I stopped the line again and said, "Sara. 20 push-ups. Now." and stood there with my arms crossed waiting. "Um, Brian, kiss my fucking ass. NOW. How 'bout that?" She stood there, arms crossed glaring at me. I felt like something had snapped inside me and I wasn't thinking; just speaking. I told her she can either do the 20, or I'll make the whole line do 20 because of her. She stuck out her middle finger with an extended arm at me and said, "Fuck you. Fucking make me" as she put down her drum and walked out. I felt the eyes of 38 other members staring at me. It was humiliating. I remember thinking, *Can I actually make her? No, I can't, so she called my bluff and wins. Dammit.* I cannot remember what happened after this, but I do not think I made her do anything; I just literally couldn't. I could never make her do anything if she didn't want to. She'd just tell me to fuck off and that'd be the end of it. There was a lot of mocking and belittling of me while in drumline, which would leave me hating going to it every day after school.

We shared a locker as a lot of couples did in high school, and we usually drove to school together. As the year progressed, I remember thinking how isolated I felt from the rest of my friends and how I was now in a position where whatever she said, I did without question for fear that she'd either get angry and cause a scene or the worst case scenario; she'd leave me and I'd be alone. We would always be together, and looking back, I wonder why the hell I didn't just walk away. My friends used to give me shit saying I was whipped. Maybe I was.

The Christmas Dance

For me, high school dances, prom, pep rallies, and spirit day were all things that I didn't overly care about, however I knew back then that these were milestones that I wanted to participate in because I knew someday I'd look back as an adult and be glad I did them. I still wonder if I was wrong. For our Christmas dance, I rented a limo for Sara, myself and a couple friends to go to dinner and the dance. I was all decked out in a tie and suspenders. Yes, suspenders. I'll never forget how I came into her house to see her just pissed off, stomping around because she felt she looked fat in the dress and how much she hated these "stupid fucking dances", as she referred to them. As any good boyfriend would do, I complimented her, saying she looked great and thanked her for her willingness to do this for me. Yes, "for me". I felt like everything she did that she didn't want to do, she would be doing it for me. She spent the entire evening just crabby.

We drove to Big Lake for dinner at a higher end restaurant on the lake and as we had light conversation with the group we were with, she sat there, complaining about anything and everything. The food was gross, the place was too noisy, the view wasn't very good, her dress was ugly, I mean, everything. I offered to pay, as any gentleman would, as I watched her walk out the door to the limo. I caught up to her, and the one thing I remember her saying was, "I cannot fucking wait until I'm 18 so I can buy cigarettes. Then I can smoke and do whatever the hell I want to and nobody can say a fucking thing about it." My heart sank. I hated when she acted like this and I could physically feel the emotional pain. I remember thinking that all I wanted was to take my date to this dance and create a memory. What I was getting was a memory, but not at all one that I wanted to remember.

When we got to the high school, Sara refused to dance. She disappeared and I found a good friend of mine to hang out with for a little while. When I did find Sara, I asked her to dance, and she did, but not until she complained about her dress, the way she looked, the stupid fucking dance, and how shitty I was as a dancer. I sometimes look back and wonder why I just didn't give up.

Drumline Rehearsal Breaks

Because Sara and I were in drumline together for 3 years and she already was able to control me by this time, I couldn't tell her no, and I could never tell her how I was truly feeling. She would always bark at me, make me feel guilty for "hurting her feelings" and we'd end up fighting. It became more difficult when my younger brother, Steven, joined. I was a senior and Steve was in 8th grade. It was his first year and not only did he not know anyone, but I was told by my parents to kind of keep an eye on him, you know, to make sure he had everything he needed. So many times, we'd get a lunch break on Saturday morning rehearsals, and Sara would say, "Let's go" and we'd get in her car and leave for lunch. Never once making sure Steve had lunch or a ride or anything. I would tell Sara, "We need to take Steve also" and she'd just say, "We don't have room; he'll be fine" as we had her, myself, her little brother and two friends with us. I didn't know what to say without causing a scene or a fight in the car with the others in there, so I was quite. I remember many times Steve never got a lunch because he had no one to give him a ride anywhere. He'd sit in the practice room and just wait. I didn't find this out until many years later. I'm not sure I will ever forgive myself for those times that I cannot take back. I think this was the beginning to the major fallout between my brother and I. That, in itself, is an entirely different story.

The truth is, I never looked out for my little brother, mostly because by doing this, it would cause tension between Sara and I and I didn't want to deal with that, or have her break up with me, even though that was probably what was needed. Sara did not like Steve, and was not going to do anything to help him. So many times I was told, "If you don't like it, leave." I felt completely controlled. I didn't think twice about what it was doing to my brother at the time, but I can't change that now. I would see Sara making sure her brother and sister had food at meal time, money if they needed it or a ride when people were leaving. I was not able to give my brother the same luxury. I never knew if he got food, I never knew if he had enough money in case he needed it or had a ride to get anywhere. I just left with Sara. I can honestly say she had turned me in to a complete asshole.

Sara's Babysitting

Sara had this family that she used to babysit for all the time. They were from her church and had two little girls. They were very Christian and had pictures of Jesus Christ all over their house along with books like "The Children's Bible" for their girls. They were incredibly sweet people. They'd call for Sara to baby sit and immediately it was assumed that I would be going along to hang out with her. Sometimes I didn't mind, if I didn't have anything else going on, but more often than not, I didn't want to go. I would tell her to go and I'd see her later or the next day. That wasn't good enough. Somehow, Sara would always find a way to guilt me into going over with her. I would find myself doing most of the work; cooking, cleaning up after, reading stories to the girls and picking up the toys once they went to bed. After the girls would go to bed, Sara and I would just sit on the couch and listen to the clock tick, or she'd read a magazine while I sat there until the parents came home. Time after time it became more and more boring for me and I grew frustrated every time I'd have to go. Anytime I would say that I didn't want to go, Sara got angry and made me feel like complete shit, so I'd feel guilty, give in and go.

It was hard because like I said, the family was very nice, so I didn't want to come off like I didn't like their kids or anything, but I just had so many other things that I usually didn't get to do that I wanted to do instead. I do remember there was one time that I told her I wasn't going, and didn't go. We had a fight about it and Sara told me she didn't want to see me after or even the next day. She said she "needed time away from me." I later found out that the parents asked why I wasn't there and she had told them she didn't know why. She told them that I just told her that I didn't want to come here anymore. It became very awkward when we'd cross paths at church or in general because for a very long time they felt like I was some asshole, and I didn't know why they were acting distant towards me until many years later, I approached them in passing to clear the air. They spilled everything that was said. All of it was a complete lie.

Don't Drive Angry

As we would take turns driving with each other to school, there was one or two instances where I would pick her up in my 1984 Chevrolet Citation; a manual transmission. She hated that car. She would always tell me that she didn't want to ride in such a "fucking piece of shit, ugly-ass car". I remember having a blowout at school, standing right in front of our lockers across from the commons. I cannot remember what caused it, or what it was even about, but I do remember trying to calm her down and keep her quiet because our classmates were beginning to look at us as they passed by. I was completely humiliated, and made some comment about how she can talk to me when she calms down. I remember walking away down the hallway to class and her slamming our locker door and storming the other direction with my classmates heckling me as I walked to class.

After school I didn't see her at our locker which was strange. There was a note saying, "Have fun walking home, asshole". I remember thinking, "Whatever" and walked out to my car. Sara couldn't drive a stick, so I wasn't overly worried about her leaving me there. Much to my surprise, my car was gone. Somehow Sara had figured out how to drive it and left me there. I remember calling her asking her where the hell she was and she replied, "At home, like I said I would be, have fun walking home, you fucking asshole" and she hung up on me. "Home" was her parent's house. That's where she was, and that's where my car was. I was very frustrated as it was January, but I began to walk anyway. It was probably close to 1½ miles from the school to her parent's house. By the time I got there, I was freezing, not to mention incredibly angry with Sara. All I wanted to do was get my keys and go home, but as I went up to the house, I could see her through the glass in the door, sitting at the kitchen table holding my keys in her finger. As I walked in she said, "Looking for these?" I just grabbed them and began to leave. She said, "Next time you decided to be a complete prick, just remember I know how to drive a stick now! Hehe…" I didn't say a word. I just got in my car and drove home.

I'll Never Have Sex With You

Tensions were high and Sara and I were having one of our many ongoing arguments about sex, again. This was frustrating because realistically, by this time in our relationship, we had been dating for a few years, and had not had sex, or any element of it. We were driving to her parents' house for dinner, and we spent the ½ - ¾ mile drive going back and forth about why we don't have any sexual side to our relationship. The fact was, she didn't like kissing-with or without tongue-holding hands, any type of touching, or any type of sex. She said it all disgusted her. She would tell me that if she were to even consider performing any oral sex on me, I would have to completely shower, wear a condom and use flavored lubricant or she would not even think of doing it; even then it would be gross.

She did not like having me do anything to her, so our relationship was similar to, well…friends; shitty friends, but friends nonetheless. We would hold hands occasionally, but rarely in public, and when we would kiss, or "make out" it was a few seconds of pecks on the cheek or lips; very rarely with tongue, and if it did involve tongue it was, according to her, "only because I'd been hounding her about it". For me, I was a growing man in my late teens approaching my twenties, and my sexual desires and mood were quite high and I was ready to try new things and experiment a little as any normal guy would be.

We argued often about how she felt the male anatomy was disgusting and just plain gross, and she'd ask, "How could any woman be attracted to a penis?! It's gross, weird looking, and has nasty shit that comes out of it. Makes me wanna vomit." Trying to soften the abrasiveness of her, I would comment and compliment her body and anatomy telling her I would love to try things with her, and just as we were pulling into her parent's driveway, she looked over to me and said forcefully, "Stop asking me to give you blowjobs! Stop asking me to have sex with you! I AM NOT going to have sex with you, and will never actually *want* to have sex with you! I'm sure the day will come when and if we get married and want kids that I'll have to have sex with you to get pregnant, but out of enjoyment, I will **never** have sex with you. Maybe I'm asexual, I don't know, but you can stop wanting it from me, it's not going to happen." I felt completely emotionally beaten, not to mention about an inch tall as I felt like a child getting scolded by their mother. She had humiliated and embarrassed me and I sure as hell didn't want to go into her parent's house for dinner now, but we were here and parking. I wanted to go home. She continued, "I'm not a lesbian, but I don't like men; I don't like either in that way. I'm not sure why, I just don't. If having sex is important to you in life, then you'll have to either deal with not having it, or leave. I'm not going to change and you sure has hell aren't going to make me." For the sake of argument, I softly agreed and said, "No, its fine. I understand." I apologized for pushing the want for sex and told her I would never ask for anything to do with sex again. I knew sex and intimacy were extremely important to me and there was no way I could go the rest of my life not having any participation with it, but she had me stuck. I told her I was fine without it, and continued on with our already poisonous, monotonous relationship.

Siblings

I thought Sara's anger and daily frustration was because of things that I did, hell sometimes I thought they were because I was just here; breathing; living. I soon realized her anger was with anybody that didn't conform to her demands. She was a controlling, manipulator and absolutely had to control the situation or people in it. I remember once or twice when we were at her parent's house, Sara, myself, her brother and sister would all be in the living room helping her mom clean, and once Sara and her brother got into it. They began arguing about who knows what and one thing led to another and she called her brother a fucking asshole and in turn, he yelled back calling her a stupid bitch inches from her face. She took a swing at him, punching him in the upper arm and he retaliated. He spit at her, hitting her right in the face and she jumped on his back, choking him and kicking his legs. It was very uncomfortable watching this. Her mom came in the room yelling at the both of them begging them to stop as I pulled Sara off her brother.

She landed on her feet, turned around and punched me in the arm three times saying, "What the fuck are you doing?! God damn it! Do not ever fucking do that again, Jesus Christ, Brian!" Shocked, I told her I hated seeing that and if she was going to be like that I was going to leave. She came up to me, inches from my face, and pointed to the door, saying, "Who the FUCK is stopping you? Huh? Go, walk out the fucking door if you're going to be a little pussy." I wiped her saliva from my face. I was so angry at her for the way she treated me at that moment, especially in front of her family. I was humiliated. I told her as I passed her that she needed to get some help, which made her snap. She took both her hands, and shoved me into the wall and said, "Get the fuck out of my house." I got my shoes on and left. I got to the car, feeling the tears coming, and drove away.

It's 8 A.M.
This hell I'm in
Seems I've crossed the line again
For being nothing more than who I am

So break my bones
And throw your stones
We all know that life ain't fair

But there is more of us
We're everywhere

Smoking

There was this time after High School, before college that I found out Sara was smoking. It shouldn't have been a surprise, but it was. I was always so against it. My dad smoked, her dad smoked, and she threatened once she turned 18 that she would start smoking, and she did. I remember one night on her parent's deck, we argued about smoking. I remember telling her how much I was against it and I was shocked that she would do that with the way her dad coughed and our dads both smelled like smoke all the time. She would take a cigarette out of her pack of Marlboro Lights, light it up, take a drag and blow the smoke into my face saying, "I. Don't. Give. A. Fuck. Deal with it or leave." Again, I dealt with it. Why did she control me like this?

She, somehow convinced me to try a drag. I didn't cough like you see in the movies, but I sucked in, and blew out. It didn't do anything for me. I took one drag and told her, "There, satisfied?" She smiled and said, "You're such a pansy. Smoke it for fuck sake!" I didn't want to. I had absolutely no desire to smoke, and I found the courage to quietly tell her, "I'm not sure I can be with someone who smokes. It's just not ok with me." "Well, sorry, *babe*, but if you don't like it, like I said, there's the door" as she took another puff and blew it into the night air. As history will prove, I dealt with it.

U of M, Morris

We both had graduated high school and gone on to college. I stayed home and went to St. Cloud State University and she decided to go away to the University of Minnesota, Morris. Without her here every day, it was bittersweet. Admittedly I missed her. Looking back I can't imagine why, but nonetheless I did. Maybe it was because she had controlled me to the point that I felt I needed her. Who knows, but even though I missed her, it allowed me to breathe a little. I found that while at college, there were opportunities to leave her for other women. I had, if I remember correctly, probably three or four girls interested in me while at SCSU. I would always tell them I was involved and they would always disappear. I sometimes wonder if those women were signs I should've listened to and bailed on Sara, but I was oblivious.

I would go to class and come home and talk to her on the phone. More often than not, she would make me feel guilty for not coming to see her. She told me how she had it all planned out. I could leave after my afternoon class, drive to see her, spend the night and leave early in the morning and get to my morning class right on time. Sure, in theory it sounded perfect, but the reality was it was around an hour drive, maybe a little more, one way, that I would have to drive. I couldn't afford the gas for one, and it left no time for studying because I knew damn good and well that we wouldn't study while I was with her. There were times that I did drive to see her though, and it was tough. I remember going one time; she called me and we'd argued most of the afternoon and on into the evening and by 9:00pm, she had guilted me in to coming to see her. I had an 8:00am class the next morning and my parent's argued with me telling me to stay. Even my dad got stern and said, "You're staying right here, you're not going anywhere tonight." I ignored them and left at 9:00pm headed for Morris. I pulled the whole, "I'm 18 and you can't stop me" card. Dumbass.

I got there sometime after 10:00pm after smoking half a pack of Camel Lights and driving like a lunatic. Why? I have no idea; I just did. Maybe frustrated at the situation, maybe because I wanted to piss her off enough so she wouldn't make me come again; I don't know; either way it was stupid. When I knocked on her dorm door, she seemed excited to see me, but was pissed that I had smoked, as I figured she would be, but it was ok, because I was pissed that she made me drive over an hour at 9:00pm on a weeknight. Besides, wasn't it her that had pressured me to start smoking? Just because she decided to stop smoking didn't mean I had to; even though I was not a 'smoker'. We ordered Pizza Hut's "The Big New Yorker" pizza and had a couple beers and hung out. Her roommate was gone for the evening, so she told me, "We have this whole place to ourselves, and you know what that means!" as she winked at me. I faked my excitement, because I knew she was referring to sex, but I wasn't stupid, and I sure as hell wasn't going to get too excited. I knew nothing was going to happen; and I was right; nothing did happen. The next morning, we woke up and I realized I was already running late. She told me to stay the day and skip class. I told her I had to go and she got pissed at me saying I never do anything for her and she has no clue why we were still dating. She threw a few insults at me as I walked out the door ignoring her. I left her dorm room feeling like complete shit and regretted even going in the first place. Needless to say, I missed my 8:00am class because I made it to school at 8:40am. I was so pissed at her and swore I'd never stay the night again.

How did I get here
And what went wrong
Couldn't handle forgiveness
Now I'm far beyond gone

I can hardly remember
The look of my own eyes
How can I love this a life so dishonest
It made me compromise

Michelle

Sara met Michelle when she left U of M and attended St Cloud State University. Neither of them wanted to live in the dorms, so they got an apartment on the North East side of St Cloud where I spent a lot of time, including unofficially moving in after a few months. Michelle was 19 years old, tall, attractive, had an hourglass figure and was an avid swimmer. She had short blond hair, piercing blue eyes, and a smile that would stop you in your tracks. She was gorgeous, and I knew I would have a difficult time spending any amount of time there when she was around, but I gave it an honest try. As soon as Sara got home to the apartment, she'd call me and I'd come over to hang out. Almost like clockwork, Michelle would be home within the hour after class or work, and we'd all hang out together. I remember Michelle's boyfriend was a Marine out of state at training and she would make comments often that she missed him. While hanging out here and there, I noticed whenever I was there and Sara wasn't, Michelle would be very friendly with me. Honestly, I enjoyed her company. She didn't treat me like shit. It was strictly platonic. When the three of us were together, Sara started noticing the way Michelle was acting around me and once we all went to bed one night, as I would spend the night here and there, Sara approached me.

"So, do you like Michelle?" My mind raced. I wanted to say, "Yes, I do. She's hot, she's sweet and I want to dump you and date her." I was 19, but I wanted to live to see another day, so I denied it. "What? No, not at all, why?" She told me she noticed Michelle gravitating towards me more and more lately and me being very friendly with her. I told her I was just being nice and there was nothing there. We went back and forth for almost an hour, arguing, her becoming angry and raising her voice. She reminded me of a few days prior where I was doing an oil based painting of some mountains and wilderness and Michelle was watching me and commented saying, "Wow, you're absolutely amazing" and how I smiled and thanked her.

I shook my head at Sara and said, "You're being ridiculous! I smiled? So because of that, I supposedly have feelings for her?" Sara told me as she glared at me, "Ya know what, I know how you work. Why don't you just go into her room, whip your dick out and fuck her brains out. Maybe then you'll get it out of your system and stop being such a fucking prick." She rolled over and went to sleep telling me to just leave her the fuck alone. I sat there trying to process what just happened, and quite honestly, I started wondering what would happen if I called her bluff and actually did what she told me to do. Go into Michelle's room. Naw, I'll just lay as far away from her as I can and try to fall asleep, I had to work in the morning, so I was getting up early. I couldn't believe how much of a left field explosion that was.

The next morning, I got into the shower to get ready for work and I heard a knock on the door. It was Michelle. She asked to use the bathroom. I said, "Sure, c'mon in." My heart racing, I prayed Sara would continue to sleep and not wake up to find this, even though nothing was happening. Michelle came in and used the bathroom. She was no more than two feet away from me. My mind started wandering, fantasizing about asking her to just join me in the shower, but that was asking for major trouble. I don't know what would've been worse, the wrath of Sara or Michelle's Marine boyfriend. I'll take choice "C"- neither. She left the bathroom and I finished showering and headed to work. I always wondered what would've been if I had the guts to ditch Sara for Michelle. Being a 19 year old man was hard, especially mixed up with Sara, Michelle and her boyfriend; the Marine. No thanks.

Sara and I decided to get a hotel room for the two of us, Michelle and her boyfriend for New Year's one year because Michelle's boyfriend was coming home. I had a co-worker friend of mine grab $40 in liquor for us and we basically drank, hit the hot tub and took turns going to the room for sex throughout the night. Well, Sara and I didn't have sex; we just talked, well, she complained about Michelle and I listened. I'm sure Michelle and her boyfriend had sex though. I remember feeling very jealous of him. He was a big muscular dude, so for the entire night, I made damn sure I did not even glance at Michelle. If I did, I would have him and Sara all over me. We didn't actually spend the night there though. Something happened between Sara and Michelle and Sara got pissed and came up to me and said, "C'mon, we're leaving" and we left. I had no idea why, and I was bummed. It didn't matter, what Sara wanted, Sara got, no questions asked.

Rocket Ride's First Show

Sara and I were just hanging out when the phone rang. It was Scott from the band "Rocket Ride". I had just gotten hired by the band to be their new drummer. He said they had a spot to play at a bar in St. Cloud and would have to head over there in an hour. I was so excited to finally be playing in an actual professional band that I said, "Sure!" and went to tell Sara. She was shocked that I said yes. "Don't you want to stay here with me?" I told her I'd love to, but I was going to be playing in a band, on stage; in front of people! She said if I stayed and didn't go, we would have sex. I knew she wouldn't so I dismissed that comment and continued to get ready. She began making advancements and became very sexual towards me, taking off her clothes trying to get me to stay.

I finally told her, "They called me to play. I'm going to play. I'll be back when I'm done and if you still want to, then we can have sex, or do whatever." She became angry and said, "Go play in your little band and be a fucking rock star. I'm not coming. I'll be here, alone, waiting for you to come back whenever you feel like it. Don't hold your breath on the sex or 'whatever', that offer only stands now, well not even anymore because you decided to be such an asshole. Have fun; buh-bye" and she slammed her bedroom door. I stood on the other side in shock. I remember thinking, "whatever" and turned, got my shoes on and left for the show.

The Proposal

I had been hearing from Sara for months that we either needed to get married or break this off. That "we've been doing this long enough and we need to decide what's next" and how she wasn't going to "waste her life away in a relationship that wasn't going anywhere." She told me on more than one occasion that I either needed to propose to her or she was going to leave me for another man, a "real man", who would want to marry her. I should've said "good luck", but I was so scared I would never find anyone else and end up alone; I panicked and decided to ask her to marry me. She told me that if I decided to ask her to marry her, it would have to be romantic to prove that I wanted her in my life, so I laid flower pedals from two dozen roses in a path down our apartment hallway along with candles. It led to the bedroom where I was on one knee with a ring asking her to marry me. Kind of cliché, but I was 20 years old, and hadn't planned on marrying anyone this early, but now the ball was rolling. When she got home from work, she followed the train of flower pedals until she saw me. Her response was, "Ok, get up, I will".

She called her mom and was all excited about it and I called my mom to tell her. We sat in the apartment talking about planning things and what we were going to do when we heard a buzz. I answered the intercom, "Who is it?" "Hi, Brian, it's mom" I let her in. She came in and stood, frozen in the entry way. Something was wrong. Sara and I stood there and asked what was going on. My mom started explaining, "I cannot let you do this, Brian. I love you too much, you're my son and I just cannot let you marry her." My mom had started crying now and had a hard time speaking. Immediately, Sara went into attack mode. "What do you mean you can't *let him* marry me?!" My mom continued, "You've been so mean to him and to our whole family. You're an awful person, and I cannot let the two of you get married, I just can't." Sara told her that she doesn't have a choice and that we were over 18 and there wasn't a damn thing she could do about it. My mom replied with, "Well, that's true, so if you're going to move forward with the wedding, then Dad and I aren't going to be there. I can also tell you that Grandma and Grandpa won't either, or your brother. No one from our side will be there." Sara, with a snarky smile said, "Fine. That's your decision; now get the fuck out of my house." My mom leaned in and hugged me saying into my ear, "I love you and I pray you'll do the right thing." And she left.

I fell apart; I collapsed right there on the dining room floor. Sara told me to get up so I went to sit down in the living room and cried so hard. How had my life brought me here? This was not how things were supposed to work. Sara had called my life long best friend and he came over to sit with me, trying to calm me down. Sara told me that my family wasn't going to be there because they were all jealous that we had found true happiness and they wanted it. I was not supposed to worry about it. She said they'll come around and when they do, she told me they'd apologize and everything would be alright. I believed her.

The Rehearsal Dinner

We had the rehearsal at the church and the dinner to follow. My brother, Steve, who was the best man, had a high school football game on the same night and he told me he could come to the rehearsal, but would have to leave to get to the game. Sara was livid. She believed he should've missed this game for us, and because this was our wedding, the world needed to stop. My brother was not one to take anyone's shit, so he and Sara got into it frequently. After many arguments about the rehearsal, Sara said, "Fine. Come to the rehearsal, then leave."

Everyone was supposed to be there at whatever time it was (the exact time escapes me), and were supposed to dress up nice. I wore dress pants and a button up, I think. My brother showed up late because of his pregame warmups for football and was wearing his entire football gear. Sara saw him walking in the door and looked at me and said, "What the fuck is your brother wearing?! Go tell him to change, now!" I approached him and told him Sara wanted him to change. He explained that he tried to leave football a few times knowing he was going to be late, and finally had to tell his coach he had to leave. He said he had no time to change and apologized profusely. I relayed all this to Sara who told me to have him change or he was to leave. I told her we needed him and he was just going to have to wear what he has because he had to play right after this. She continued to complain about how he was going to ruin all the pictures and we'd look back and think how much of a hick wedding this was going to be. I hated her for putting me in the middle of her and my family, which was quite often. I remember her finally saying, "Well, if the world has to revolve around Steven, then by God, we better all bend over and take it up the ass, huh? Jesus-fucking-Christ, Brian, you are such a dick. Whatever." I remember thinking *Oh, God don't let anyone see me get emotional right now.*

We went on with the rehearsal and as soon as it was over, Steve told me he had to go and was already late. I was so pissed at Sara and generally crabby with how the whole thing played out and I snapped at him and told him to just go. He left feeling like shit, I felt like shit and Sara told me, "Karma's such a bitch, and it'll come back to bite your brother in the ass someday, and I'll be there to see it." My heart broke. I just wanted this night to be over, but we still had the dinner to get through. God help me.

The Wedding Day

Ah, the wedding day. A day that most people cannot wait for. A day when two people who are madly in love with each other get to profess their love for one another. A day that signifies the beginning of the rest of their lives as one. For me, this was just another day in hell. Sara and I got married because it was the next step in our relationship, not because we were in love and couldn't imagine life without one another. I hardly think there was any "love" in our relationship. We liked each other at best. We arrived at the church for pictures, and I remember them going alright, so, I'll get to the actual ceremony.

I remember my dad was on edge. He didn't seem relaxed or happy at all, but I was too blind to see that then. My mom would smile at everyone and thank them for coming, but thinking back to that day, I know her smile was forced, because that was the polite thing to do. Both my mom and dad walked me down the aisle to the front. I had chosen my only brother, Steve to be my best man. We hadn't been getting along and really never spent any time together, but I wanted him as my best man because he was my brother; my only brother, and I knew someday I would look back and know I made the right choice. To have him as my best man was a point on contention between Sara and I because she had one brother and felt very strongly that he should be my best man. This was one of the only times I actually stood my ground and told her, "No, Steve is going to be my best man and I'm not going to change my mind" she told me, "Well, I think you're making a shitty decision, but what the hell do I know? Your brother is an asshole. Always has been, always will be. I have no fucking clue why you would pick him, but whatever" as she would flail her arms about. Despite our differences in, well everything, to this day, I do not regret that decision.

The music cued while I stood there and watched my soon-to-be wife walk down the aisle with a smile. A very forced smile. Almost like the kind of smile and facial expression that one should have under these circumstances, not one of pure enjoyment. We went through the service, said our vows, and exchanged the rings. The priest proclaimed us Mr. and Mrs. Brian Morgan and everyone clapped. At the time, I was excited because I was married and life, real life, could begin. We headed out and to our reception which was held at a nice hotel in St Cloud. I guess, looking back the wedding didn't go too bad, but the reception led me wishing the day would've just gone away.

The Wedding Reception

We watched everyone trickle in and take their seats as we took our seats at the head table. My brother was sitting next to me and Sara's sister next to her. We just sat down when the clinking of the glasses started and I looked over at Sara with a smile and she rolled her eyes, stood up and gave me a peck on the cheek. We got some light hearted "Boo's", so she stood up and said, "Ok, we will give you three kisses. After that, we're done. Someone else can kiss, or no one can kiss. It's our wedding day and we will be eating." I think that set the tone for the rest of the evening. Not even another minute later, more clinking. I looked at Sara, ready to pucker up and she leaned over with another peck. I whispered to her, "Are you going to kiss me at all?" She whispered with a glare, "I am not going to fucking make out with you in front of all these people. I did kiss you. If that's not good enough, kiss someone else." I felt this wave of heat come over me and prayed that no one saw her chew my ass just then. As far as I was concerned, I was done with her right then and there. I had shut down and I didn't even want to sit next to her, or dance with her, or even spend the night with her. I wanted to go home; alone.

More clinking. She looked at me and under her breath said, "Well…say something." I stood up and said we were done kissing and asked who wanted to take this kiss, waiting for a response. I saw a crowd of straight faces and not much of a response. This was awkward. We continued to eat until we started speeches. I cannot remember who went first between Sara's sister and my brother, but I do remember each speech being weird. I think they both tried to say something similar to what you say at weddings, but both struggled. Maybe it was because they were both much younger than us. My brother was 18 and her sister 17 at that time, so who knows.

The rest of the dinner and dessert was a little blurry in my memory, but I do remember the dance. We did the traditional first dance, then the wedding party dance, and father/daughter, mother/son, etc. I remember people dancing for a while until the music wasn't really working for people to dance to. People started fizzling out or sitting down, or just hanging out. The DJ was playing to maybe 6-7 kids and that was it. Sara came up to me distraught saying, "Do something! No one's dancing and people are starting to leave." I walked up to the DJ to see my dad talking to him. He had a microphone in his hand. I turned and went back to Sara who was standing there staring at my Dad. "He is NOT going to sing at my fucking wedding." What was I going to say? Was he? Of course he was. He had a microphone and had a few drinks and there was no one that was going to stop him. He started out with Bob Seger's "Turn the Page". After the first song, it became like a karaoke request hour. People were leaving and Sara was livid. I think if her head could've exploded it would have. She pulled me aside just outside the dance floor and began screaming at me to "get your drunk ass dad off the fucking dance floor and send him the fuck home. This is not a fucking rock concert, it is my wedding!!!" Sara's mom threw her hands up as if to say, "It's over, nothing I can do" and walked down the hallway heading to their room. Why couldn't I just disappear?

I approached my mom and explained the situation. From what I understand, she talked with my dad, who was offended and ended up leaving. The DJ attempted to change up the song choices, gearing them more towards the dance music people could dance to, but it was too late. The majority of our wedding guests had already left. Sara was stomping around the place, barking at her mom, dad, sister, brother; anyone in her path. She came barking at me, pointing her finger in my face saying, "I hope you're fucking happy. This was your fucking fault that everyone left. You can't control your fucking parents and now look what happened. God, what a great fucking wedding day. You have no fucking backbone, do you? No; I didn't think so" and she walked away. I remember standing there, watching her walk away wondering what the hell I got myself into, and realizing I'd never seen her this mad before. Her face was actually red with anger. I just literally married this person. She was my wife, and I would be spending the rest of my life with her. Wonderful.

The Wedding Night

We were exhausted, angry and frustrated from the day and were heading back to our suite as a newly married couple. We were told our room was on the second floor of the hotel on the far end. Sara walked in front carrying her train and I followed with our two suitcases. We got lost. We couldn't find our room and Sara was getting pissed. She kept saying "Where the fuck is our room?" I kept telling her that I could go back to the desk and get better directions, but she insisted I not leave her just standing here alone, and she refused to come back to the desk with me. "We'll just find it ourselves" she said. My arms were killing me as I was pulling two large suitcases in one hand and carrying coats and her two small bags in the other. I suggested we just leave the suitcases along the wall for a minute and walk by ourselves until we find the room, then I'd come back for them. She asked if I was stupid because I suggested that. She said, "Then what if someone steals them? Are YOU going to replace everything that gets stolen right now tonight? I think not". Our arguing was continuous until I dropped the bags and said, I'm going to find the room and I left. Not 5 minutes later, I found it and returned for the items-still there.

We entered the room and saw it was the honeymoon suite. Immediately, even after the day we had, I began to think about having sex with my new wife. The fact that we were now newlyweds became very apparent and I remembered that she'd always wanted to wait until we were married before we had sex, so this was to be our first time. The entire day had faded away. It was all about what was going to happen in the next five minutes. I began to be romantic and massage her shoulders hoping one thing would lead to another, but what happened next was unexpected. I should have expected it, but for some reason I didn't. She stood up, got out of her dress, put on pajamas and climbed into bed. She turned off her lamp and said "goodnight". I stood there in half a tux wondering what the hell just happened. I got undressed and climbed into bed with her. I rolled over next to her and put my arm around her to hear, "Uh, no. You're going to need to give me space, and put on some pajamas; you're not fucking sleeping naked next to me; gross". I told her I thought we were going to have sex tonight as it was our wedding night, and our first time. She said, "I'm tired and not in the mood, but if you absolutely have to get off, wait until I'm sleeping, then either do whatever you want to me or just jack off, I'm going to sleep. You could give me a backrub if you wanted to, I could use one." I remember sitting on the edge of the bed thinking, *are you fucking kidding me*? She could kiss my ass if she thought I was giving her a backrub after the way she treated me the last 24 hours. I got out of bed, put on my pajama pants and shirt, climbed back in bed, rolled over and hugged the far end of the bed feeling completely ashamed and humiliated. I laid there feeling this wave of anger, sadness, embarrassment, frustration and awareness that I was officially married and still a God damn virgin come over me. I debated on just moving to the couch sleeper for the night, or staying where I was, but fell asleep before I could make the decision.

The Honeymoon

We went to Duluth for our honeymoon and stayed at Thomson House historic bed and breakfast. Even though the wedding night didn't end with some sort of sex or intimacy, at this point I didn't care. We were on our honeymoon and I was sure things would change then. It's a honeymoon, and what else did people do on their honeymoon but have a lot of sex, right? At least that what I thought. We arrived and found our room, dropped off our stuff and decided to go hiking. We found the Congdon trail just a block off of where we stayed. We hiked it for about an hour before we weren't sure where we were. Nothing looked like it was supposed to and neither of us was for sure that we'd get to where we needed to go, and the frustration began. I cannot remember exactly what was said, but I do remember feeling a lot of pressure to figure things out. I didn't know what to do, and on top of it all I had to pee. We were the only two people for as far as I could see and hear, so I went to find a tree. "What the hell are you doing" she asked. I told her, "I can't hold it any more, I have to pee." "I cannot believe how much of a fucking hick you are. You cannot piss here; this is not a fucking bathroom, God!" I ignored her as I relieved myself. I wanted to turn back to where I knew an opening was and just get out of the trail and back on the city road. Sara didn't want to do that. She wanted to just figure it out. We continued on the trail for a while longer, arguing and fighting. I was called many names including "worthless", "piece of shit", "fucking idiot" and the list went on.

By the time we did realize where we were, I was able to let my guard down a little and breathe a sigh of relief. I was emotionally hurting and wanted the day to just be over. We walked back to our car in silence and drove back to our room in silence. By now, the weather had changed and it was raining. We got up to our room and she said she wanted soup and a sandwich for dinner and wanted me to go pick it up. I agreed simply because I just wanted to leave for a bit. I already needed a break from her. I drove down the hill to the restaurant, and parked. I had to walk about a block to get to the front door. I grabbed the food and walked back to the car. I was drenched, but didn't care. When I got back up to the room, she was lying on the bed reading. We ate in silence until I finally spoke. Looking around the room, we had a fire place, and a hot tub/shower built for two. I said, "Look, this is our honeymoon. We have a nice featherbed, a fireplace and a hot tub for two. Let's get a little creative." She wasn't keen on the hot tub idea, but turned on the fireplace. We tried having sex, but didn't go so well. It was very awkward. She was giving me instructions and critiquing everything I did. It shouldn't have been that difficult, but every position or move I made either was irritating or annoying and she'd tell me to "stop it" or ask "what the fuck are you doing?" After about 20 minutes of being ridiculed and critiqued, I lied and said I was tired and I rolled over and tried to fall asleep, feeling the emotions build and the tears fill my eyes. "Don't get pissed at me when we don't have sex anymore because just remember this was your decision to not do it. I finally agree to have sex and you fucking give up. Christ." She got dressed, grabbed her book and finished reading. Someone pinch me.

The next morning, we went downstairs for the breakfast part of the bed and breakfast. That was weird because she was not a people person. Light conversation took place, but anytime any questions were directed towards us, Sara would kick my leg and I would respond. She didn't want to talk to "these people" as she informed me later. There was a living space there where some of the other guests would gather to socialize with some wine or other sort of liquor. We would be invited to join and socialize, but Sara would tell me before we left our room that we were NOT going to stay around this place and talk to these people. I didn't know really how to handle this. I never wanted to be rude, so I'd try to make up an excuse as to why we weren't staying, but my lying was shitty, and I'm sure it showed. We spent time down by the pier the second day and couldn't spend more than 15 minutes without Sara complaining about something. It was exhausting. I wanted to tell her to just shut up and try to enjoy herself, but two things weren't going to happen; I wasn't going to tell her to shut up. That would most likely lead into World War III, and my untimely death, and she wasn't going to enjoy herself. Doing anything outside of lying on a bed with a book was too much to ask.

That evening we talked and tried a clean slate. We decided to utilize the two-person hot tub/shower and see where it led. After awkward positions and getting frustrated with her endless complaints on everything I was doing, including the water being too hot, then too cold, my penis; everything, I got angry and grabbed my towel and called it quits. She then got pissed at me, saying it was all my fucking idea to have sex in there. She told me, "You don't have any fucking clue what you're doing, do you? I'm not going to be your guinea pig. Figure your shit out, and let me know when you know what the hell you're doing." I felt about an inch tall. I wanted to crawl into a hole and never see her face again, but there I was, standing in only a towel facing her, dripping wet. I remember apologizing to her and said that I would not ask her to have sex again. I remembered saying those words before.

I told her I understood I didn't know what I was doing because I had never been with anyone in this way before. I said she wouldn't have to worry about any more awkwardness. I was done asking, hinting, initiating and trying. She laughed at me sarcastically saying, "You? Stop wanting sex? Ha! Good luck with that! I've heard all this shit before, ya know. You're a sex addict and can't seem to live for even a single day without either annoying me with your sexual advances or jacking off. It's disgusting." I felt the tears roll down my cheek. As the insults and nasty words kept coming, so did the tears. I remember trying so hard to hold everything in so she wouldn't see my weakness, but I just couldn't. My chest felt tight, I had a wave of heat come over me and lost control of my emotions. I had no strength left to hold it all in. She had hit me again with the low blow. We had been together now for roughly 5 years, we were married, on our honeymoon and hadn't had sex yet. We'd tried a few times, but never really had sex. I was 21 years old, married and still a fucking virgin. So frustrating. After the comment she made, I quickly got my pajamas on and told her to go fuck herself and climbed into bed, trying to stop crying. She replied, "Go fuck myself? Really? Get the fuck out of this bed. I'm NOT sleeping with such a fucking asshole. You can sleep on the floor or in that fucking chair" as she pointed to a chair in the corner of the room near the fireplace. I chose the floor.

Drummer Needed

My good friend, Scott from the band *Rocket Ride* was a guitarist filling in for a band up in Ogilvie, MN which was probably 45 minutes from where I was. It was about 10:00pm, and Sara and I were in bed. The phone rang and it was Scott asking if I could come fill in for their drummer. His hand had cramped up and couldn't finish the night. Scott said I'd get paid really well. I told Sara I was going to go fill in for this guy and bring home some money, and I could tell she was frustrated, but said, "Whatever.", so I told Scott I'd be on my way. I was so excited to be playing but I was stupid because I took highway 95 straight East at 10:30pm at around 90 mph in the Saturn. I flew around a curve to watch the car that just passed me hit the brakes and turn around in my rear view mirror.

Within seconds, I saw the flashing of red and blue lights. Shit. I needed to slow down, obviously, but didn't want him to see me braking, so I just downshifted from drive into 3rd, and then into 2nd to let the engine slow the car before I was at regular speed, then I braked. I pulled over and had to provide my license to the officer who asked if I knew why he pulled me over. I told him I wasn't sure. He gave me a smile, turned and went back to his squad car while I sat there with two thoughts running through my head. One, I'm going to be super late to play for Scott's band now, and two, when Sara finds out about this, I'm dead.

The officer returned and asked if I knew how fast I was going. With my heart up in my throat, I said, "67…68 maybe". Completely lying, I know. I thought the speed limit was 65, so I figured that would sound legit. "93" he said. "93 miles per hour in a 55 mph zone. That's 38 miles per hour over the speed limit. Do you have any idea what that means, son? That could be considered a misdemeanor, and you can appear in court in front of a judge and explain why you were in such a hurry. I can take your license and give you a nice ride to jail in my squad, maybe have your wife come pick ya up if you're lucky." I begged him not to do that, insistent that I was well under 70 mph. I told him my cruise was set at 66, and I was singing to the radio and had no idea I was going that fast. Thinking of how Sara is going to kill me, I found a way to work up some tears and show some panic. He looked at me and said, "Maybe your foot was resting on the pedal causing the vehicle to accelerate… Here's what I'm going to do. I have to write you a ticket, there's no way around that. But that's it. I'm gonna cut ya quite the break here." He began writing and told me to slow down, reminding me if he catches me again, it will be jail time. I thanked him for understanding, asked to shake his hand and I took the $82 ticket and finished the evening out playing with Scott and his band. The first song we played once I was on stage was Judist Priest's "Breakin' The Law." Pricks.

I drove home that night at between 54 and 55 mph to find Sara still awake in bed reading. "So, how much did you make?" Not sure what to say, I said, "$80 bucks". "That's it?! I thought you said you were going to get paid well." I told her for two hours of playing that was pretty damn good. On average, I'd play a four hour show and get maybe $75-$100, so $80 for two hours was damn good. I told her there was one problem. I told her I got pulled over and got an $82 ticket. I held my breath, and felt my heart in my throat waiting for the atom bomb to detonate. She was livid. I think I was called every name in the book; Sara was just screaming and swearing at me. She made me get the phone and call Scott, who was still at the bar. She made me ask for more. I argued with her because it was not at all the mature thing to do, not to mention completely humiliating. She wanted the price of the ticket covered and for us to make a profit. I begged her not to make me call him. It was so degrading. She forced me to, as she screamed obscenities at me, inches from my face. I just prayed the neighbors couldn't hear.

I called and asked, trying not to cry. My voice was shaky and I was holding back falling apart. The whole time I was talking to Scott, Sara was in the back ground yelling at me, telling me what to say and not to forget to say that I needed it tonight. She would make me call every 5 minutes. Every time I'd call I'd say, "Hey Scott, I'm sorry to call again, but I really can't avoid it. I need to know." He kept saying he was trying but had no answers and would call me when he knew something. I hung up. Five minutes later, I had to call again. I wanted to die. I told Sara that Scott would call me, she said, "I don't fucking care; call him NOW!" Scott ended up talking the band into pooling some of their payout to cover some of the ticket price. Because it didn't cover it completely, I had to live with an extremely pissed off wife for the next two solid weeks. I didn't understand it, because it wasn't like we needed the money. We were sitting at roughly $5,000 in the bank at that time.

Sandstone, MN

When I was playing with *Rocket Ride*, we had to play this show up in Sandstone, MN. I took my parent's motorhome because it was a Friday and Saturday night show, so I wouldn't be coming home in between as it was just too far away. I packed a cooler full of beer and some Capris Sun juice pouches. I wasn't thinking clearly, obviously. I remember having no money. She had "allowed me" $20 for the night and the entire next day.

We set up for the show at around 3pm and waited around drinking until show time. I spent a lot of time arguing on the phone with Sara for most of the day and into the evening, mostly about money and how I didn't have any, and needed some, and her telling me I should've packed more food and how I was a dumbass for not doing so. I do remember our arguing ended with us yelling at each other, her hanging up and me throwing my phone across the motorhome.

Tommy, one of the guys in the band, walked in at the last few minutes with a beer in his hand and after I threw my phone, he handed me an un-cracked Budweiser and said, "I get it, man, let's just drink" and we did. Tommy and I drank one after another after another. Soon Scott came in with a beer and joined in. The three of us drank and talked all the way up until 9:00; showtime. I could hardly see straight once I stood up. Everything was spinning, and I couldn't walk or talk for that matter. For lack of a better term, I was completely fucked up. I took the stage with help from my two good friends and Tommy, nearly fell off my drum chair twice before even starting, and played the first set. I used the bathroom on our first break and when I exited, I saw my two best friends who had come up there with me, along with Tommy talking to this small group of college-aged women.

I don't remember any of them except for one. She was very attractive. Brunette, shoulder length hair and wearing grey leggings tall brown leather boots. Tommy was telling her that I was their drummer and incredibly talented at *many things*. Basically trying to hook me up with her. I kept telling him "no man, I'm married, I can't" but he leaned into me and whispered in my ear, "Hey, I know what you're going through and I'm not trying to fuck any of that up, just trying to have you enjoy yourself for one night. I ain't gonna say nothing and neither is

Scott." I looked over at Scott shaking his head, and tipped his beer at me.

This woman who we referred to as "Grey pants" was putting it on pretty thick and I was playing into it; and why wouldn't I? I was completely plastered and felt like I had nothing to lose, not to mention hadn't even tried having sex in what, two…three years? I had a show to do and was attempting to focus on walking back to the stage. I do remember this woman grabbing my arm as I walked away, pulled me back close and said if we played 3 Doors Down's "Kryptonite", then maybe I'd get lucky after the show as she winked at me with a smile. I told her I would make sure we would play it, and would play it just for her. I wasn't going to tell her that that particular song was played every night anyway. Sara was the furthest thing from my mind at that moment. Grey pants was quite possibly just another sign I should've followed. After that set, I couldn't find her anywhere, but it didn't matter because I was completely exhausted, pissed at the fight Sara and I had earlier and was just ready to go home, but we had a whole day and night to do tomorrow. With my world still spinning, I tried calling Sara during that last break to try to make amends, but got no answer. Probably a good thing considering the shape I was in.

I Want a Baby

We had found out that Sara's dad had cancer, and after the initial conversation was over and Sara had finished crying, we spent the evening as we usually would by lying in bed, reading or doing crossword puzzles. I remember we were in the midst of moving, or soon to be moving, and she looked over at me and said, "I want a baby. I don't want my dad to die before he gets to meet his grandkids." I remember having this conversation while at our first house, but when we were trying, we were in our new house. I remember talking about trying to get pregnant and how we'd do it "tonight". We did our nightly routine and climbed into bed. All day I'd been waiting for this moment and I was excited. We were going to have sex, and I'm not even sure we'd actually had sex yet. We were going to have some bedroom time together, which was so very few and far between. Lying in bed, she turned the TV on and started flipping through channels.

She was lying on her back with her legs crossed, and all I could think about was having sex and trying to get her pregnant. I began getting close and kissing her neck, letting my hand wander and trying to get her in the mood, but nothing seemed to be working. I began thinking of giving up because I started feeling stupid that here I was trying to have some foreplay, and was getting completely ignored.

It was hard to ignore my racing thoughts of all the things I must have been doing wrong and focus on getting her in the mood to get pregnant. Various things I would try, caressing her breast, or running my hand up her thigh, would end with her shrugging me away saying, "Stop that, it's annoying." I think my attempts must have gone on for 30 minutes before I finally gave up. Frustrated, I rolled over and lay there, pretending to watch TV with her. Trading Spaces. Nothing says, "Ooh baby I want you" like Trading Spaces on TLC. My mind was racing. I was wondering if I should say something, or if she was going to say something, or if I should just lay there watching TV, or roll over and go to sleep. I was going crazy. We hadn't done anything intimate together in months. Not even simply kissing. Tonight was supposed to be special. Tonight was supposed to be memorable, which it was becoming, but just not in the way I had hoped.

We laid there next to each other, but seemed worlds apart, silent, not saying a word. Out of nowhere, she said, "Well, are we going to have sex and get me pregnant, or not?" I replied, "I've been trying to get you in the mood for the last 45 minutes, and you don't seem like you want to." We went back and forth with little arguments about who was or wasn't in the mood, and whose job it was to make this happen. She then said to me, "Well, you need to get yourself hard and let me know when you're ready to cum, then I'll let you cum in me." This was not how it was supposed to work. Something didn't seem right and now with the way things were, I was not remotely close to even wanting to be in the same room as her. I wanted to leave. I felt quite degraded and about an inch tall. This hot wave of emotion washed over me and I wished I was anywhere but there. I lay there trying to process what just happened in the past 45 minutes and while I was sitting there speechless, she interrupted my thoughts saying, "Well? Are you gonna get yourself hard or not, or can 'cha get it up? Haha.."

I remember lying on my back staring at the ceiling feeling a mix of wanting to punch her in the face and trying not to cry; feeling my chest tighten up. Ah, that familiar emotional heartache once again. I was completely humiliated. "Well?" Sara said as she's now on her side facing me, with the look of impatience on her face; eyebrows raised. "I don't wanna piss the whole night away." She pointed at my crotch, "C'mon, pull it out, jack off and get hard. . .now. C'mon." I told her I could use some help and asked if she wanted to give me a blowjob or touch me, or something; anything, and she replied, "Ha! Ah, no, thanks, I'm good! That's not my job! Besides, the male penis is disgusting; that's all you." I was so frustrated and felt so degraded, but something snapped inside of me because of all the humiliation I felt and I very sarcastically said, "Ok, fine. Here ya go." And I pulled my pants down, grabbed my penis and started aggressively stroking it saying, "There, ya happy now? I'll take care of it, don't worry, I got it…" I felt myself began to cry a little, but tried like hell to hold it back. I hated her for making me feel like this. I hated myself for not standing up to her. I didn't want her to see me cry because all it would do it trigger more humiliation and ultimately end in another fight; a bigger fight. I had very mixed emotions and quite honestly didn't know how to handle any of them at that moment.

As one can imagine, the situation I found myself in was not at all enjoyable, and was next to impossible to live through. She would tell me that I needed to knock it off and get serious because if we didn't have sex, she wouldn't get pregnant, it would be *my* fault that we would never have kids and that's not something that she would accept. We lay there together, her insisting we do this right now tonight and me having given up long ago. I would much prefer that we just forget about it, and try again another time, but that's not what happened. Needless to say, I did manage to find myself successfully able to get hard by nothing less than a lot of praying and begging to my internal self to just make it happen, "Please, please please, just get hard. Please help me get through this, please…" All I wanted was to get this night over with.

By now, she was back watching TV and I told her I was hard and told her we could have sex. She looked over at me and said, "I didn't say to let me know when you were hard, you were supposed to let me know when you were ready to cum. I'm not going to have that huge nasty thing sliding in and out for the next 5 minutes." Up until this moment, I didn't know I could feel any more humiliated than I already had, but apparently I was wrong.

I spent the next few minutes masturbating more, and praying to myself more to just hurry up and get there. Finally I said, "Sara? I got myself up to where I would be able to cum. . ." When I told her I was ready, she said, "Ok" and allowed me to climb on top of her while she continued to watch TV. It lasted only seconds and it was over. I came. "Are you done yet?" she asked me. I hated the way I felt. I quietly nodded yes and rolled off of her and laid on the bed facing away from her. My chest and heart was killing me from my emotional pain. It kept clenching up and made it difficult to breathe. "See, that wasn't so hard, now was it?" she said as she flipped through the channels on the TV.

Trying to have a baby was supposed to be enjoyable and memorable, and it was nothing of the sorts. It was embarrassing, degrading and left me feeling plain shitty; but it was over. I remember lying there hoping we'd get pregnant so I wouldn't have to re-live everything that happened. As far as I was concerned at that moment, I never wanted to have sex with her again. She'd won. All these thoughts were running through my head while I laid there feeling used. We ended up getting pregnant.

I remember for quite a few months after this, I did not want to even touch her, I didn't want to be next to her, I just wanted to co-exist. It wasn't as hard as I thought it'd be because we rarely kissed anyway, and holding hands never happened either with her, so all I had to do was avoid the intimacy in the bedroom, which didn't exist anyway, and I'd be fine. For once, I felt good being simply alone and married. I'm sure there was more to what happened before I fell asleep that night, but somehow it's been lost in my memory most likely never to surface again, the rest of it, unfortunately I will never forget.

My name is worthless like you told me I once was
My name is empty 'cause you drained away the love
My name is searching since you stole my only soul
My name is hatred and the reasons we both know

Worthless, empty, searching, hatred
Well who am I right now?

You're fuckin' wearing me out!
You're always dragging me down!
You're the fake, fallen, force of nature, sick mind
I don't need a gun to take back what's mine
It's over
It's over now
You're done wearing me out

Shattered Dreams

While I was playing with Rocket Ride, I had heard on the radio that one of my favorite bands were coming to Minneapolis, and were looking for an opening act. What you had to do was record your band playing a couple songs, then send the tape in for a chance to be chosen to be the opening act. We had an outdoor show coming up, so I figured it was perfect. I can't remember exactly who videotaped us, but that is irrelevant at this point, but we set up and played our show in front of roughly 100-150 people on a beautiful summer night. The part of the video I sent in was one of our better songs, a drum solo, right into another song. I sent a letter along with the video asking that the video be returned, as it was the only copy I had; which I never got back. Needless to say, we were not chosen, but something did come of the tape…

I was at home, and I remember it was a sunny afternoon because we had all the windows open. I cannot remember what we were doing, but I want to say we were cleaning the house, or doing laundry, or something similar when the phone rang. Sara had gone outside to hang clothes on the clothesline and I answered the phone, "Hello?" I said. "Yes, hello, I'm looking for a Brian Morgan…" I told the man on the other end that I was Brian Morgan and asked what this was about. He informed me that he was from an agency based out of New York City that worked with musicians or bands of national status and wanted to know if I was the drummer he saw on a video tape submitted for a contest. Immediately I didn't know what to think. Part of me thought it was a joke, but my gut told me this was no joke, this was really happening. I told him that I did send in a video of my band playing a few songs for a contest to open for a band coming to Minnesota, and he told me that he was sent the tape from a colleague who handles promotional advertising for touring bands. He told me he was impressed by my playing and wanted to offer me a life changing opportunity. I stood in the dining room next to our table staring out the window as he explained what he does. He said he finds musicians and pairs them with bands, or solo artists needing a band and basically that's it; then you're on tour with whomever. He mentioned as an example that if Taylor Swift needed a band, he'd build one from the various musicians he had access to; including me. Like, I could be the touring drummer for Taylor

Swift…for example. He asked me if I was interested in pursuing this opportunity and having my life changed forever.

I didn't quite know how to wrap my head around all this. For me, I was just a 20yr old drummer from central Minnesota. I was no "rockstar". Was I interested? Hell yes I was, but I would have to talk to Sara about it first, after all, we were married. I told him I was very interested, but I would have to discuss it with my wife first before I accepted. He said he would give me 24 hours. He explained that if I accepted the offer, there would be a one-way ticket provided to me for the flight to New York. There would also be a place to stay, free of charge, until I would become established and find my own place. He said they would have a drumset for me, and all I'd have to do is get on the flight, and just show up; he'd take care of everything else. Before we ended our call, he reminded me that I had 24 hours and to realize that this would be a once in a lifetime opportunity for me. He gave me his direct office number, and I told him I would call him by tomorrow evening either way. I thanked him for calling and hung up.

I stood there with the phone in my hand, staring out the window, reliving what just happened. What *did* just happen? Did I seriously just get offered my dream job?! "Who was that?" I heard coming from behind me. It was Sara. I tried to contain my excitement, but it didn't work. I blurted out, "A guy from New York wanting to hire me as a professional drummer for touring!" She replied, "No, seriously. Who was it?" My smile went away, and I repeated it, "Seriously. It was a talent agent from New York. He saw the tape I sent in and wants to fly me out and offer a career in drumming professionally to me. Like, I would tour with high end, famous artists. What do you think?" "What do I think? I think you're married to *ME,* and we're beginning to start our family. I think this is a pipe dream of yours that is pretty fucking far-fetched if you ask me. I think you made the decision to be a family man, not a fucking "rockstar" a long time ago, you can't just say, 'Meh, I wanna be a rockstar' and ditch your wife, dog, house, and life just to go play band with *some guy* who tells you he's gonna do all this shit." I stood there feeling shaky, numb, almost emotionally unstable. What was happening? As I stood there, with all these questions running through my mind, Sara continued on talking at me. "What do you want to do?" I froze. *Was I supposed to answer this question truthfully?* I took a deep breath, and explained to her, "Sara, this is something I've wanted my whole life, and never even fathomed that it would ever happen, and somehow it has. This is my dream to do this, and I have an opportunity to actually do it. That doesn't happen to very many people. I would really like to go." She began laughing. "Do you have any idea how stupid you sound? *'It's my dream! I've wanted this my whole life!'* " She continued to laugh. I could feel the tears begin to surface, but I held them back. My heart and chest felt tight and I found it hard to breathe. She continued talking until I finally spoke and said, "So, that's it? I have to say 'no'?" She stared into my eyes and said, "Yes. You're not going. You're not doing this. You're a family man, not a fucking rockstar, it's time to grow up."

I spent the next day at work trying to find a way to ignore what Sara said and go anyway, but by the end of the day, I knew there was a call I had to make. Sara wasn't home yet from work, so I sat down at the table, and pulled the note with his number written on it. It felt like an eternity the amount of time it took to dial the number, but I dialed it. I remember a woman answering, saying, "Hello, (so & so's) office, how may I direct your call?" I cannot for the life of me remember his name. I want to say it was Steven, or Mark, or some other simple, bold name, but I just can't remember it, anyway, I asked to speak to him. She asked me who I was so she could tell him who it was. I gave her my name, and she replied, "Ah, yes, the drummer. Just a moment..." I remember thinking, *God this sucks. I do not want to say no...* "Hello?" came the voice of the man I spoke to yesterday. I told him I had no choice, but to decline the offer. I don't think he was expecting that, I remember a pause, like he didn't know what to say, nor did I. I explained that I spoke to my wife, and she was not on board, so I had no choice but to decline I will never forget his response, "You do know, you may never get another chance at this, don't you? I'm offering you a golden ticket to all your dreams, to play in front of thousands of people every night. You're sure you're going to pass on this?" My heart was racing, and my hands were sweating. My mind was screaming, "NO! NO! NO! I want it!!! I'm coming!!!" but my voice quietly said, "Yes, I'm sure, thank you for the offer, but I have to pass." He thanked me for the time and wished me luck in my future endeavors and hung up. That was the last time I ever spoke to him, and the last time I was ever offered anything with that magnitude. He was right, that opportunity never did come around again.

Send away for a priceless gift
One not subtle, one not on the list
Send away for a perfect world
One not simply, so absurd
In these times of doing what you're told
Keep these feelings, no one knows

What ever happened to the young man's heart
Swallowed by pain, as he slowly fell apart

That's Why We Don't Have Sex

I remember one of the few times we attempted to have sex, and the insults and degrading comments followed, we laid there in silence. I remember her saying, "Do you want to know what I think?" I laid there shouting out endless answers to that question in my head. *"Because you're a bitch? Because you'd rather make me feel like shit? Because I'm just your sperm donor?..."* Did I want to know? Hell no. I wanted her to just shut up for once, but I didn't get what I wanted. "I think your penis is not at all normal." I looked at her with the most confused look on my face and asked, "Are you kidding me right now?" She said, "No, seriously, have you ever looked at it? It's not perfectly straight, and that's a big problem. Have you ever talked to anyone about it?" I quit listening because I kept hearing her first comment play over and over in my head wondering if it actually just happened.

"I think you should go see someone; seriously." I heard this comment over and over in my head as well. I had never been with anyone else, so I didn't know any better, and I began to wonder if maybe she was right. I'd seen porn before, so compared to other's I felt I was perfectly normal, but now I have my wife telling me I was broken. For some crazy reason, I believed her. "I think that's why we never have sex" she said. "You're too big and because you're not exactly straight, you can't have sex with women. You probably need to have it straightened out and made smaller." My mind was too full of all this crap to even understand what the hell was going on at that moment.

The next day, she continued on with the conversation and somehow convinced me to call the Urologist and have an appointment set up to have myself looked at. I didn't think there was any problem, but because Sara seemed genuinely concerned about it, I believed her. I went to the appointment, and endured the humiliation of getting aroused and letting the doctor inspect me. He told me there was absolutely nothing wrong with my penis whatsoever. It was like any other he's seen and not every penis is completely straight. He said I had nothing to worry about and my wife should be happy with what I have.

I came home and told Sara what I was told and she immediately said, "Who'd you see? He sounds like a quack. I think you should get a second opinion." I told her I was not getting a second opinion and if she didn't like my penis, then she didn't have to deal with it. I was fine with the way it was, so I wouldn't be looking into it any further. Still, Sara continued, "I would love to have a healthy sex life with you, but cannot when your anatomy is so messed up. Have you ever thought about having it surgically altered so it was straighter? We could have sex all the time then!" I knew full well, even if I had exactly what her opinion of the perfect penis was, she'd never have sex with me *all* the time. It would be few and far between at best. I became angry with her because none of this was necessary. It was humiliating, degrading and embarrassing, and I wanted to be done with it all. I told her I was done talking about it, and she said, "Fine. If you want to live with a fucked up dick, then you can enjoy jacking off with a crooked dick then; it's all you" and she walked out of the room. I remember thinking, "Jesus, what the fuck is she on?"

The Breast Pump

Sara tried breast feeding Michael after he was born, but for whatever reason, he just wasn't attaching, and it wasn't overly successful, so she was told to get a breast pump and just pump. She had a friend that had one, so she just borrowed hers. I didn't understand why we wouldn't just go buy one. By this time in our marriage, we had anywhere from $5,000 to $6,000 in our checking account at any given time, but Sara didn't want to. She didn't want to "piss away" any money. The pump she got worked fine for a while until it was 1:00am and she was trying to pump.

I remember one night, I was sleeping and the next thing I knew, I was being shaken and tapped on the shoulder. It was Sara. "Get up. Are you awake? I need you now" and she left the room and headed back downstairs. I was completely out of it. I had no clue what was going on, only that something was wrong. I came to my senses, grabbed my glasses and flew downstairs. The living room light was on and Sara had a kitchen chair with a TV tray set up in front of the TV. She had the pump sitting on the TV tray and was trying to pump. She very angrily told me that the pump would run, but wouldn't suction. She showed me as she brought the suction part up to her breast and held it there. Sure enough, nothing was coming out. She threw it across the room saying, "This thing is such a fucking piece of shit." I stood there, glanced at the clock seeing that it was 1:12am. I didn't know what she wanted me to do. I knew nothing about these things and didn't know how to get it to suction and actually pump.

I asked her, "What do you want me to do?" She stood up, got in my face, pointed to the pump assembly and said, "Well, for starters, why don't you try to fucking fix this piece of shit!" I told her I had no idea even where to start. She picked up the motor, shoved it into my chest and said, "Well, ya better fucking figure it out and fast. I need to pump and this needs to work, so fucking DO SOMETHING!" I frantically began looking at how to open it up. Tiny screws; perfect. I went to get a small screwdriver and began opening it up. "What the fuck are you doing?!" she yelled at me. I told her, "If you want me to try to fix it, you need to let me try to fix it." "This isn't even ours!" she screamed. "You can't start just ripping into it! Jesus Christ, Brian. You really are a fucking idiot!" I ignored her and continued tearing into this thing.

Once opened, I turned it on and found the problem. The rubber seal inside wasn't sealing; therefore it wasn't getting any suction. I thought if I could get it to somehow seal, it would work and she'd relax. I couldn't access it though; my fingers were too big. I showed what I was looking at to Sara and explained what needed to happen. I asked her if she could try because her hands were smaller. To my surprise, she said, "No, this isn't my fucking problem." She continued to complain about her boobs hurting and demanding I hurry. I remember sweating, and my hands shaking by this time. I kept getting sweat in my eyes and they'd burn, so I'd try to wipe the sweat away, and continue working on jamming my hand in this contraption. I was able to barely get my two fingers around this seal and lift it up. I got it! I put everything back together and watched Sara pump to make sure it worked. It did. The motor was running and it was actually pumping. She said, "Jesus Christ, finally. Now it's 2:15am and I'm just now pumping. So much for getting any fucking sleep tonight." I glanced at the clock again, yep, 2:15am. I leave for work at 5:30 tomorrow...well, today now. I told her I was going back to bed. I did not wait for a response; I just left, wiping more sweat from my forehead. I climbed back into bed and fell asleep.

3:00am, I woke up to the sound of Sara screaming my name from downstairs. I grabbed my glasses again and flew down the stairs. "It's not fucking working again. What the fuck did you do to it?" I ran through everything I did the last time, and told her it probably wasn't going to work, and we'd have to just buy a new one tomorrow. She said, "The fuck we will. You're going to fix it again, and now, so get crackin'".

My emotions were running so high I was fighting tears and trying to bite my tongue. I was so extremely tired, but I got my screwdriver and opened it back up. Same thing. I jammed my hand in there again, this time something cut my skin across my knuckles. They began to bleed. Sara said, "Don't get blood all over this, and remember it isn't ours." I just glared at her. "Do NOT fucking glare at me. If you would have fixed it right the first time, you wouldn't have to fix it again. This is because of your stupidity." I ignored her and continued jamming my hand as far in as I could to try to reach the rubber seal again.

I began to cry from frustration, her insults and being very overtired. For some reason, her words cut like knives and after enough insults, she broke me. I kept praying in my head, "Please God help me fix this, please God help me, please…" I got the seal again and lifted it up to where it needed to be to get the suction again. I turned on the pump. It worked, it sucked. Sara grabbed it out of my hand and brought it up to her breast. "Good, it works again…for now." I told her I was going to go back to bed to try to get some sleep. She said, "Ah…I wouldn't get too comfy. This'll probably quit working again, and you'll have to fix it…again." I told her I don't know how many times I can try to get it to work in one night. I told her it was old and used and we really needed to get a new one. She gave a sinister laugh and said, "Fuck that. You'll fix it if it quits working, and that's the end of it." I walked away up to bed. The next thing I heard was my alarm clock, and noticing Sara sleeping next to me. Thank you, God.

I wonder if the things I did were just to be different
To spare myself from the constant shame of my existence
And I would surely redeem myself in my desperation
Here and now I'll express my situation

There's nothing ever wrong but nothing's ever right
Such a cruel contradiction
I know I crossed the line, it's not easy to define
I'm born to indecision
There's always something new, some path I'm supposed to choose
With no particular rhyme or reason

Poor Excuse for a Man/
Escaping Death (The First Time)

I cannot remember how our paths crossed, but I became emotionally involved with this girl from Florida named Liz. She and I had some things in common, but not everything, enough to chat and have some conversation. One thing led to another, and I ended up having an emotional affair with her. She was never coming up to Minnesota, and I was never leaving Sara to move there. She made me feel good and showed excitement when I shared things with her. We'd chat almost every day and for long periods of time throughout the day. With Sara's ongoing nastiness, I felt so low that I turned to others to feel good, hell, to feel like a human being. Liz kept me somewhat sane in an insane marriage.

Because things were the way they were between Sara and I, and had been for quite some time, and because I had been talking to Liz, our cell phone bill was high; ridiculously high. We had a minimum shared minute plan with virtually no text messaging. I had used hundreds of minutes and many, many text messages talking to Liz and everything showed up on the statement. I was at work in Minneapolis, and my phone rang one afternoon. I answered it to hear Sara screaming at me on the other end. I couldn't understand a word she was saying except for multiple vulgarities and insults. I hung up. Seconds later, she called back screaming again. I told her I couldn't understand her and what I got out of the conversation was that she knew what was going on and started asking me about who's number was (whatever it was) and why I had racked up some ungodly amount of minutes. My actual answer to this question escapes me now, but I remember telling her something, other than the truth. Her response was that I was to go to the nearest Wireless store and have them credit our account what we were charged over the normal bill amount. I told her there was no way they would, but she insisted I do it. Her exact response was, "you're going to fix it, or don't bother coming home." So I went in-had to do something.

I talked to a sales person, explaining the situation, and was told what I figured would happen. I used the minutes, I pay the amount due. I even talked to a manager, same thing. This wasn't rocket science; I knew we'd have to pay the bill. Realistically, I found myself in a nasty catch 22, which would inevitably leave me screwed one way or another. I left the store and as I was walking to my work truck, my hands shaking, I called her. I explained how I tried to fix it, but was told no. She yelled and yelled and said, "I cannot believe how pissed off I am at you." I apologized profusely, but it didn't matter. She told me again, "I told you that you either fix this or don't come home. You didn't fix it, so you better find a place to stay tonight. You're such a fucking poor excuse for a man. God I fucking hate you right now. I know I'm pissed and I really don't give a shit. Deal with it or leave!" She hung up. By this point I was crying. I felt sick to my stomach and the sun was going down. I didn't know what to do. I didn't know where to go. I called her mom. We talked a little and I told her I had nowhere to go and asked if I should stay there. She said she didn't know what to tell me, and didn't want to get in the middle of this, so I responded with, "I'll figure something out" and hung up.

...Somethings wrong with you I see
Your eyes have turned a shade of empty
In my arms you pushed aside
Wondered if you'd ever be
Alright again and try to fix
What's going on inside of you

I remember driving towards home after my shift. I got into St Cloud and it was getting dark. Sara had called me three or four times while I was driving, and I would let it go to voicemail. I didn't want to talk to her. I was scared of what she would say, what she would tell me, I was already sick to my stomach for having to deal with all this for the past couple hours. I hated myself for even feeling scared of her. Scared of my wife?! Scared of a woman?! Yes. I was scared of her. She was unpredictable and God only knows how she would react to me not answering my phone. Would she change the locks and prevent me from coming home? Would she attack me when I walked in the door? Would she do something to me in my sleep? My mind raced and wandered and I began to panic. I didn't want to go home, but was scared of what would happen if I stayed away. I became frazzled and confused and was just about to lose it when she called me; again.

It rang two or three times just as I was coming into town. I decided to answer this time. "Hello?" I cannot tell you what she said because it was all yelling and swearing. Endless insults and degrading comments. With tears in my eyes, I didn't think; I just hung up and threw my phone across the car. It landed on the floor between the passenger seat and door. It rang again. I didn't know where I was going; not home, that was for sure. I turned onto Hwy 23 from Hwy 10, and headed out towards my parent's house. I thought, *I can't go there. How would I explain what happened? I don't want to explain.* I ended up turning off onto a county road behind the main drag and saw nothing but open county road and fields. There were a few power line poles, and some trees, but that was about it.

Suddenly things all slowed down and something became clear. I said a prayer asking God to forgive me for what I was about to do, and to not have anyone mad at me. I unbuckled my seatbelt, pressed the gas pedal into the floor and let go of the steering wheel and closed my eyes. I was crying as I pressed myself back into my seat and kept thinking of what was going on outside my closed eyes. When would I leave the road? How fast was I really going? The engine pitch was high, so I knew it was far past the speed limit. If I left the road, would I just get hurt, or would I kill myself? Would the car roll, or flip, would I be ejected or just tumble inside of it, scrambling my brains? When will I feel the impact? I didn't want to live through a nasty accident. I didn't want that pain. I wanted to hit something like a tree or a power pole, or something. Something that would completely destroy the car and me. Something to bring the car to an immediate stop, sending me through the windshield, killing me. Anything to kill me quickly, with little to no pain. I feared the immense pain if I didn't die or became paralyzed and that scared the shit out of me. I was bawling by now, and immediately panicked. *Oh shit! What the hell was I doing?* I thought as I stomped on the brake pedal and opened my eyes.

The sound of the tires screeching on the pavement was eerie, as the car came to a stop; dead center of the road. I looked around and noticed I had only gone maybe a quarter of a mile. It seemed so much longer. My heart was pounding in my throat and I was shaking uncontrollably. I thought I was going to throw up. I pulled my car to the side of the road and put my hazards on. I sat there, bawling, with my head against the steering wheel thinking of what I had just done. I was going to actually kill myself because of a fight I had with Sara. Because of many fights I've had with Sara. Somehow I couldn't quite wrap my head around it. Furthermore, I had closed my eyes, put the gas pedal to the floor and let go of the steering wheel… and drove in a straight line? There were no cars to hit, no wildlife, nothing. That was strange, almost creepy. I just sat in my car on the county road and fell apart onto the steering wheel. I cried so hard and prayed that this heart wrenching pain would go away. I prayed that I would find the strength to survive another day with Sara. I'm not sure where I went after that. I find it hard to believe that I actually went home to her, but nothing is certain.

Escaping Death (the second time)

Sara and I had gotten into another huge fight, shocker, I know. What it was about this time, I cannot remember, and is beside the point. I remember leaving the house despite her actions to stop me. I remember her calling me names, very nasty names with her finger inches from my face, and threatening to change the locks if I left, but I left anyway. I needed to cool my head. I remember having the sensation of living in a prison without the ability to breathe. I got in the Saturn and just drove. I drove around in circles, up and down random streets crying, yelling at the steering wheel, outwardly saying everything I wanted to say to her, but only to my windshield. I kept driving until I ended up at a park overlooking the river. I turned off the lights and sat there thinking. I cried, felt the hatred towards her and re-lived what just happened. I could hear her screaming at me in my head over and over. It wouldn't stop.

This was another one of the few times I tried taking my own life and just being done with everything. I just didn't have the energy or emotional strength to continue on. I thought of different scenarios that would do it without causing me any pain. Last time scared the shit out of me, and nothing guaranteed that I would die quickly. There was that chance that I'd live and be paralyzed or feel some level of pain. The way I saw it, I had lived with enough pain for the past few years that I deserved to die quietly. Just let me go. I had no gun, I couldn't fathom hanging myself and the struggle and panic that I would feel; where I would do it, or most importantly, who would find me?

I started looking around the car for a way to cause some level of physical pain to eliminate the high level of emotional pain I was feeling, and found my pocket knife. I took it out, and opened the blade. I considered stabbing myself or slicing my wrist like you see in the movies, but both of those options scared me, and wouldn't guarantee a quick death and more pain; a lot more pain. Searching further, I found a bottle of pain medication. It wouldn't eliminate the emotional pain, but maybe if there was enough of it, I could take all of it, and I'd just pass out and never wake up. It seemed plausible. I knew nothing about what it would do, being pain meds, or even if it would kill me, but with my emotions high, and so much hatred and anger towards the person I was in prison with, I wasn't thinking clearly, and I just swallowed whatever was in the bottle which seemed to be a little more than a dozen pills. I sat there bawling like a baby, saying prayers in my head over and over, asking for forgiveness from God first, then asking God to please let my family know I was sorry, and begging them not to hate me for what I did.

It didn't take long, and I can't remember what triggered me to come to my senses, but I panicked and immediately got out of the car, got on all fours on the ground and shoved my finger down my throat aggressively to try to throw up the pills. Nothing was happening and I began to panic more saying to myself, "I don't wanna die" over and over. I kept jamming my finger as deep as I could, then I felt a rush of hot acid come up. I puked.

I sat there on all fours on the ground sobbing and apologizing to God for being so stupid, then thanking him for saving me. I remember it wasn't too late in the evening, but it was dark and somewhat secluded where I was, so I figured no one would see me, and I hoped nobody would. As I looked at what I threw up, I saw a handful of blue pills in the mess. The sight of that made me cry even more. I felt so low. I wondered how the hell I got here. I was a good person dammit. Why was I living in this hell? Why did I deserve this? I hated myself. I managed to pick myself up and get back in the car. I sat there and tried to calm my breathing and get my composure; I was shaking and my whole body ached.

I checked the clock, and realized that I had better get home before I was in some real trouble. I wiped my eyes, which were completely bloodshot and red. I remember thinking that Sara was going to see me and question why I was crying and God only knows what was going to follow that whole discussion, so I had to try to get rid of the redness. She hated when I would cry. When she noticed tears, that's when the real degrading comments started. She was good. She'd push me emotionally over the ledge until I would show any sign of crying, and then off would come the gloves. It would make me so angry. I hated her for doing that to me.

I drove home in silence and pulled into the garage. I sat there for what seemed like an eternity. It must have been only a minute or two, thinking what would happen if I put it in reverse and just left? Just drove and never came back. What would happen? Naw, I better go in, or I'll be in some deep shit. I quietly came in, all the lights off and quiet. I went upstairs to our bedroom to see her in bed. I whispered to her, "I'm home". She replied, "You're sleeping on the couch downstairs." I turned and went back downstairs and grabbed a blanket and laid on the couch. I remember feeling exhausted and crying as I fell asleep, my mind re-living the past hour.

Bouquet of Flowers

After the second attempt at suicide, I woke up the next morning and went to work like any other day. After work, I stopped by the local floral department to pick out a bouquet of flowers to give to Sara and apologize for our fight last night. I wasn't sorry because I didn't feel like I had done anything wrong, but I had learned that if I just take the blame and apologize for whatever started the fight, we would make up and move on with our lives, so I became good at saying I was sorry. Anyway, I went in to the store and spent a decent amount of time looking through all the "cash and carry" flowers. I remember thinking that if I went that route; I would have to find a vase at home, arrange them and present them to her without her knowing-not going to happen. I decided to go to the more expensive section where everything was in a vase and arranged. I found a dozen roses with greens and baby's breath. I thought it was perfect. Big, bold, and fresh. I went to pick out an "I'm sorry" card and read through about a dozen before I found the right one that professed my love for her and said exactly what I wanted to say.

I drove in the driveway and saw Sara standing at the kitchen sink through the window. I smiled, and she just turned away. My smile faded as I grabbed the bouquet of flowers and card and walked in the house. She had left the room so I set the items on the kitchen island and stood there for her to return so I could apologize. She walked in the room and said, "What the hell is this?" I began to explain how I was sorry for the way things went last night and she interrupted saying, "Roses? Seriously? I fucking hate roses, and YOU know that!" Shocked, I told her I wanted to get something that was bright and bold and that showed my love for her. She said, "Where did you get them?" I told her "The local florist". She replied, "Well, you can return them and get your money back because I'm not going to have fucking roses in *my* house. God, you just don't have a fucking clue, do you?" as she walked in the living room shaking her head in disgust. I stood there speechless. My heart ached. I walked in the living room and attempted to apologize for the flowers, and again she interrupted me saying, "I'm not kidding. Take them back and get your money back. I'm not going to waste, what? $50 on some fucking ugly ass flowers. Put your coat back on, take the flowers back to the florist and get your fucking money back. Now."

I put my coat on, grabbed the bouquet and card and got in my car. I walked into the florist and up to the courtesy counter to see, of all people, my cousin working the counter. Completely embarrassed, I approached her, explained what happened and told her I had to return these, as I handed the dozen roses to her. She looked at me and said, "Don't worry about it, I get it. I'm sorry". She discreetly scanned the flowers, and issued a refund. I left the store feeling the eyes of a dozen or two people staring at me. I got back in my car, managed to hold back the tears that were coming and drove away. I got back home, and threw the card in the garbage as I went upstairs to change clothes.

The Treadmill

When Sara and I were financially comfortable, and she wanted a treadmill. She constantly complained about her weight and said if she had a treadmill, she could use it every day and really get into shape…for me. We shopped around and found a Pro-Form II one that was pretty nice. We got it home and I brought it into the breezeway. "Ah, what are you doing" she asked. I thought that's where it was going, but I was mistaken. She wanted it upstairs in the opening in the hallway. We went back and forth with how I felt it was not going to fit because there just wasn't enough room up there for it, and she insisted there was. Her request turned into a demand and eventually I had no choice. I was bringing this heavy thing upstairs.

Our house was an old farmhouse with steep steps and low ceilings. It had a staircase that had a sharp 90 degree turn right away, then up eight stairs, another sharp 90, and five more stairs. I had to remove the railing so it would fit, and even then, it was extremely close, almost impossible. I asked her to help bring the back of it up, and I'd carry the front part with the motor and all the weight. I began going up backwards, bending over and pulling with everything I had. She couldn't get her end around that first sharp turn, and would yell at me to figure out another way. There was no other way. If she wanted this thing upstairs, it had to go up the stairs. We tried twisting it, turning it, flipping it; everything. Nothing was working. Sara became enraged and pressed her feet against the wall behind her and shoved with her entire body weight. She rammed it into the wall, taking out a chunk of plaster and scraping the plastic of the digital display. Somehow, this was blamed on me for being a "fucking dumbass".

After jamming it three or four times into the plaster walls, she said, "Fuck this shit" and walked away. I sat there on the upper end of this treadmill; stuck. I couldn't get it back down and start over, so I had to keep pulling. It was stuck. I was so angry, I was tearing up. I was swearing and decided to say, "screw it" and give it everything I had and fix whatever broke, later. I managed somehow to get it upright and over my head and I walked it up the stairs and flopped it on the floor upstairs. I spent the next 30 minutes reassembling it and getting it to work.

Over the next two to three weeks, Sara rarely used it saying, "I don't like it here. There's no TV and it is always in the way. I want it downstairs." Was there any point in arguing with her? I began to take it all apart; again. I propped it back up and on my shoulders and I walked it downstairs and into the living room. The rest of this memory is a blur. I do not remember what I ended up doing with the treadmill, or what happened next. That's all I have left. I did end up fixing all the holes in the upstairs walls from her jamming the treadmill into it. Touched up, re-textured and painted. Even that she complained about saying it looked like shit. Did it matter?

Light It Up

We had just laid commercial carpet in the kitchen/dining room and not two weeks later I destroyed it. Sara had made a cake and we became accustomed to "hiding" baked goods in the oven so our dog wouldn't get to it when we weren't around. On this occasion, we had brought home, if I remember correctly, take and bake Pizza. We came in, put down a few groceries we had picked up and I pre-heated the oven to 400 degrees. It must have been three or four minutes when Sara noticed a strange smell coming from the oven and light smoke coming out of the vents. Immediately, we both said aloud, "The cake!" I ran over to the oven and opened up the door to see the Rubbermaid cover completely melting and dripping on to the cake and some small flames on the element that was burning because of the melted, dripped plastic.

Without thinking, I reacted and grabbed the cake pan and cover with oven mitts, and ran it outside. It was winter, so I just threw it into the snow. As I was running out of the kitchen, some 25 feet to the door, she was yelling at me not to do that, calling me a "fucking idiot" because while I was trying to get the burning cake outside, it was dripping blue liquid plastic drops in a nice trail all over the new carpet towards the door. I didn't know this until after the fact. At the time, as soon as I opened the oven door, gray smoke flowed out, the smoke detectors were beeping and I reacted.

Now that the fire was out and the melted Rubbermaid pan was half buried in the snow, I came back in to face her, frustrated that I "ruined" our brand new carpet. I saw each blue dot of now hardened plastic melted into the carpet fibers in a nice trail from the door to the oven. Each dot maybe the size of a pencil eraser or smaller. I told her I was sorry and I would work at getting all the blue up. She just rolled her eyes, and said, "Whatever, glad to know we just pissed away a thousand dollars on new flooring that is now destroyed." She left the room and I grabbed a utility knife and got down on my knees and began to lightly scrape the blue plastic out of the carpet. Some of it came out alright; some was melted so deep that I used a scissors to snip away at some of the fibers to try to pull the blue up. I worked at this for just over an hour. At one point in time, she came into the room and said, "Do not cut the carpet." I didn't say anything except, "I won't", even though I had already snipped a few areas.

Painting the Kitchen

Married life with Sara was ever changing. Never was she satisfied with anything. Whether it be the furniture arrangement in the living room, or the color of any one of the walls in the house, to the kitchen cabinet color, or a rug color. Name something, she got sick of it within a week or two of the way it was. Every weekend became an opportunity to re-arrange something in the house. Often times, I didn't want to do it, but she would tell me "then just get the hell out of here, I'll do it myself." Like clockwork, she would work at whatever it was by herself for ten minutes, fifteen tops, before I would hear her grunting, swearing, and throwing something against a wall or through the air. Then it would be my turn to come in and fix things. There was always a project going on whether I wanted there to be or not. One of the biggest projects we did was the kitchen.

She wanted to repaint the kitchen. After completely gutting it, throwing every single element away, I had re-insulated the walls, removed a window, and installed a new window in a completely different place and redone the sheetrock. All freshly stained and varnished new red oak cabinets were installed, khaki marble countertops and a deep wine red wall color was painted. Honestly, I liked it. I never thought we'd completely change it. She taped off the walls and painted all the cabinets bright gloss white, and when that dried, she began priming and painting the walls a grass green color. We still had carpet in the kitchen during this renovation. She wanted me to help paint, but every time I painted, she would get just pissed that I wasn't painting right and tell me to leave. I would either miss a spot, or paint a light spot in the color, or whatever; always something not good enough.

This time, I was taping, she was painting. I had installed a large archway separating the 24'x26' dining room and kitchen that she was painting green on the kitchen side. I had used that blue painter's tape to tape the crown molding and the line between the green kitchen and cream dining room color. As she was brushing it on, she was mumbling and complaining; swearing about the shitty tape job I had done and how everything was going to have to be touched up. I remember standing near the doorway into the kitchen, watching her up on the step ladder painting this part of the kitchen and paint kept dripping off her brush onto the carpet. Every time it would drip, she would swear. "God damn it!" "Son-of-a-bitch!" Over and over. I would continue to tell her that "I'll take care of it, don't worry" as I got out warm water and a rag or a toothbrush to gently wipe up the green spills on the khaki kitchen carpet. It seemed for every drip I cleaned and got out, there were two more to do.

I remember telling her to wait so I can get a drop cloth or something to put down, but she kept telling me that she's almost done, or don't worry about it. Drip after drip, I would wipe it down, trying to get out all the green, but no matter how long I worked at it, there was just a hint that was left that I could not get out.

I remember Sara finishing and climbing down off the ladder, just pissed at the amount of subtle green drips that I "didn't get out". Frustrated, I raised my voice, telling her if she would've just waited for me to lay something down, there wouldn't have been this issue. She yelled back, I can't remember exactly what was said; something about my shitty tape job, and I yelled back. I was frustrated. Her and I yelled back and forth for a minute or two until she snapped. I will never forget what happened next. Face to face, she said, "You think you can do better? Then fucking do it!" as she threw her paint-filled brush across the room. I watched it almost in slow motion bounce across the floor leaving three or four very significant green globs of paint on the carpet from the kitchen into the dining room. I remember raising my voice to her saying, "What the fuck, Sara!!??" She turned, got right up into my face and pointed at me saying, "Fuck you, you fucking asshole!" and with a swipe of her hand, knocked the paint tray off the island onto the floor. Thick green paint ran everywhere. She stomped upstairs to our bedroom and slammed the door. Frantically, I got out a roll of paper towel and a dust pan to try to wipe up all the paint.

I was so angry, and panicked that tears were falling out of my eyes, and that in itself made me angry because I kept thinking, I'm not sad, so why the hell am I crying. I remember talking to myself, insulting myself and blaming this entire situation on my actions saying, "I should have just shut the hell up". By this point in our marriage or *relationship*, I would often default by blaming myself for everything that happened. I learned very quickly that blaming her for anything would just end up causing more of an argument and more fighting, so it was easier, and much less abrasive to just take it and move on.

I had grocery bags full of paint soaked paper towels. I was using carpet cleaner, warm water mixed with Dawn dish soap; anything I could think of to try to get this paint out of the carpet. Nothing was working. I got 80% out, but then there was always that subtle hint of green that just wouldn't come out. I used a scrub brush also, but nothing. I used Oxy Clean; nothing. No matter what I did, there was no removing that last bit of green. When I was on my knees, scrubbing, I could hardly tell it had been there, but when I stood up, there they were, plain as day. Green marks all over the kitchen carpet, and large green blotches from the brush and entire paint tray. I was physically, emotionally, and mentally exhausted as I sat with my back against the refrigerator, crying into my hands. I didn't know what else to do, and quite honestly, I was scared of what would happen when Sara would come back downstairs. I sat there running many scenarios through my head of how it would go when she came down. She was always somewhat unpredictable. The only thing that I could bank on was that however she would react, it would be nasty. It's just how she reacted to things. I never really knew how angry she would get; that was always a surprise. My chest hurt, and I was slightly shaking. My hands, wrists and knees were cramping and incredibly sore from kneeling and scrubbing to get the paint out. It wasn't long before I heard footsteps from upstairs coming down. I remember wanting to stand up, but my body wouldn't let me, so I froze. I couldn't move.

Sara came around the corner and asked if I even tried to clean the paint out of the carpet. My heart sank and my jaw dropped. I was screaming at her in my head, but nothing was coming out of my mouth. I began to tell her what I had been doing the past half an hour, but she interrupted me saying, very sarcastically, "It's ok, sweetheart, I'm sure you tried your hardest. You know what? I didn't like this FUCKING carpet anyway!" and she grabbed my hammer off the island, and pulled away the base trim along the wall by the dining room window. I jumped up saying, "What the hell, Sara!?" She looked at me and screamed, "You shut the Fuck up!" She came back to the island, and grabbed my utility knife lying near the paint can, and walked back to the wall, grabbed the end of the carpet with one hand and with the other, she sliced the carpet with the knife. She ran the knife through the carpet from the wall some 10 feet up to where I was now standing. With the carpet sliced in two, she threw the knife down, bent over and grabbed the lifted carpet with both hands and pulled intensely. You could hear the sound of the carpet ripping as she tore it all up. She left a large flap of carpet just lying there. As she caught her breath, she smiled at me and said, "Good. Now you have another project to finish" and she went back upstairs. I stood there feeling like I was going to throw up. I felt cold; numb. I was shaking. What just happened? Is this a dream, or did this really happen? Is this *really* our dining room? The tears that had fallen down my face had stopped. I felt nothing, almost out of body. I didn't know if I should go talk to her, or leave, or just stand there frozen. I had a million thoughts running through my head, none of which I could grasp onto. What just happened? The rest of the memory is blurry, and I cannot recall what I actually did.

Pushing My Limits

Sara and I got into it again tonight about how I couldn't get the green paint out of the carpet yesterday. She had finished painting the green that still needed to get painted during the day today. Like yesterday, more paint drips without putting anything down to prevent it. I had been scrubbing my ass off, holding back tears of anger and frustration again, but I just couldn't get it out. I thought I could salvage the carpet, so I was trying to get the paint out. Almost like déjà vu, she got pissed and had gone upstairs while I worked on the carpet. It seems like every waking moment with her is a fight.

She came down from upstairs, saw me scrubbing the carpet, and the hint of green still there and lost control. She began kicking the paint cans, pushing over bar stools and yelling at me saying I "can't do anything fucking right". I was so unbelievably angry with her that I got up without saying a word, grabbed my keys and was going to leave to cool off. She ran up and barricaded the door. I told her to move. She told me I was not leaving and I couldn't make her move out of the way. I took a breath and calmly asked her to move. She could see I was angry and trying to maintain my calm. I told her I needed to leave to calm down and then I would come home. Still, she said, "no" with this matter of fact look on her face. She said if I was going to leave then I would have to physically move her as she crossed her arms and stood there, legs apart. I hated this because I was raised to NEVER hit or lay a hand on a woman. To this day, I never have and never will, no matter what, but she pushed and pushed me to my breaking limit, knowing I would never hurt her. We went back and forth about this door thing until I finally told her, nose to nose to "Get the fuck out of my way". She laughed a sinister laugh at me, and said, "Move me then". I went to grab her arms to move her and she yelled, "Are you trying to rape me?!" I froze. I could not believe what she just said. She began to laugh again, calling me many derogatory names and throwing insults at me. I couldn't make out what she was saying, but I could hear her voice screaming at me. I was almost in a trance processing what she just said. The whole time I was listening to her yelling these things, inches from my face. I remember feeling her saliva hit my face as she was going on and on. I felt my heart racing and my vision going blank. I felt a cold tear run down my cheek. I was losing control of my emotions, and now my mental control was fading. I felt my fingers on my right hand curl very tight in a fist. My forearm and bicep, I remember feeling tight. My heart raced until it was in my throat; pulsing in my ears. Her insults continued and her arms flailing. She was leaning into me, consuming the space all around me without ever touching me. I was called everything from a sorry excuse for a man, "pussy little fucking mama's boy" so on and so forth. I finally snapped.

I put my fist right through the wall inches from her head. I was not at all trying to hit her. I didn't want to hit her. It was the wall I wanted to hit. She went silent as she stared at me with large eyes. I didn't know what I had done. I didn't know I could go right through plaster and lathe through to the insulation, but I did. We looked at each other for a split second, tears in my eyes as she started laughing at me and calling me a "fucking psycho". Telling me that I should probably go see a shrink and get myself checked in to a rubber room. "Ya know, maybe get fitted in one of those strait jackets they put lunatics in." she would say. I started crying more. I was broken. I couldn't help it any longer. I felt my body go weak, and I fell apart. My heart physically hurt and I was emotionally exhausted. I felt numb. She moved out of the way and said, "There. Get the fuck out of here."

Her insults continued and went from calling me psycho to a crying mama's boy. She kept telling me she thought she married a *man*, not a fucking child. She kept her insults going while laughing as I left the house to the garage. I stood there in the garage trying to decide what to do. Do I leave? I really didn't want to because last time I left, I almost killed myself, and I was very aware that my current state of mind was the same as that last time. I knew if I left, I would most likely try something else, and what happens if this time it works? Do I stay? Yeah right, and deal with more of this relentless abuse? How much more could I take? I just stood there next to our Hyundai Santa Fe re-living the last 5 minutes, hearing her words replay over and over in my head. My anger rose again and emotional pain was unfathomable. I hated emotional pain, still do, but back then I would always prefer physical pain to emotional pain. Physical pain I knew would come to an end; with emotional pain, I was never really sure.

As I stood there, I lost it again, thinking of all the things she said continuing to go over and over and over in my head. Without thinking, I took a downward close fisted swing at the side of the Santa Fe and left a huge dent. My emotional pain was so high, I couldn't stand it anymore, and I frantically searched the garage for something to cause me physical pain so that it would drown out the emotional pain I was experiencing. I was almost hysterical, crying uncontrollably. I found an aluminum baseball bat, but I was too chicken shit to use it. I found a crowbar, but too scared of what it would do. I've seen crowbars used in movies. A nail gun, hammer, screwdriver, chain, utility knife, the list goes on. Then I found a three foot pine scrap piece of 2x4. I grabbed it and started whaling at my legs and knees as hard as I could. I hit myself about ten times before my legs were tingling and numb and I just couldn't support myself anymore. I collapsed. It hurt like hell to get up and walk, but at least my chest and heart quit hurting so bad. All I could feel was the physical throbbing pain of the strikes up and down my legs but none of the emotional pain I had been suffering. I waited until my crying subsided and quietly went back into the house ten or fifteen minutes later. She had gone to bed, so I grabbed a blanket and found the couch again, crying until I fell asleep.

It's cold outside I'm sensing fear
My self-control has disappeared
I'm spinning out at each end
Could you be kind and let me in

Despite the writing on the wall
My future's bleak and rather small
That's all you could ever take from me
I've got nothing to lose so let me be

Drums In The Closet

Upstairs in our house, there was this closet. It was roughly four feet deep, eight feet wide and seven feet tall, but the ceiling immediately slanted; the room was essentially triangular. It was virtually unusable for anything other than clothes or storage. We used it as an office, well, not even that. More of a place to use the computer with a shelf and the rest was all storage. I had wanted to set up my drums for almost a year and had nowhere to put them. It was bothering me, but I just couldn't do anything about it. Sara told me she knew how much I wanted them set up, and would try to figure out a way to make that happen.

One day, she approached me and said, "Here," pointing to the closet, "Set your drums up in here." Knowing there's no way in hell they were going to fit, I told her, "It's a good idea, but they're not going to fit." She didn't understand how the drums wouldn't fit. I explained to her that although they'd fit the length and width of the room, the height was a problem. I mentioned that I needed at least five feet of height at the front and there was only three. I told her there was no way I'd be able to play them even if I got them set up somehow. No matter what she thought of, realistically there really was no way for this to work. Finally she said, "Fuck it then. Here, I try to find a place for you to drum, and all you can do is bitch about my ideas. Figure it out yourself then. God!" Needless to say, I tried to set them up just to humor her, and they did not fit; not even close. They remained in their cases.

The Family Christmas Party

The annual family Christmas party; always unpredictable with Sara. I remember one year in particular, it was held in a conference room at a hotel in Sartell. Getting ready at home, we had been arguing almost constantly about my family and her opinion of each one of them. My uncle was a racist asshole, my dad was a drunk, my grandma was annoying, my aunt was a complete fucking idiot. I heard about each one of them from her. I would attempt to somehow try to "understand" where she was coming from-which was virtually impossible most of the time, and trying to defend my family at the same time. Her family was a complete disaster, but somehow it was perfect in her eyes. Everything relating to her was perfect, and it was always everything else that needed fixing. That was her way of thinking. Honestly, it didn't matter one way or another, she was going to inevitably push me to either anger or tears by the words and insults she was so very good at using. This time it was tears; again.

We loaded the van with some food and gifts for people. The drive there was silent for the most part until we turned into the parking lot. I cannot remember what caused the fight, but as we parked, I was taking nasty insults from her and trying not to cry. It didn't work. She knew what buttons to push and got off on pushing every one of them. I hated that I was an emotional person; more so than I had ever been. She'd spent years breaking me, and molding me into this punching bag of a person that she could use and I never could find the strength to avoid an emotional breakdown. It was inevitable. I began to tear up and gritted my teeth, trying like hell to stop it, but couldn't. We parked and she stopped and said, "Well, let's go. Wipe your tears baby boy, it's time to go in and put a smile on your face. You're not going to want to cause a scene, are you?" I wiped the tears and looked in the mirror. My eyes were red, but I got out and carried in the stuff anyway. As we entered the room, I tried to smile and pretend everything was fine, but I remember the way my family was looking at me. They knew. I remember it was tense and awkward and all I kept thinking about was how badly I just wanted to leave. I watched Sara go around to all my family members, giving hugs with a smile on her face saying "Merry Christmas!" I wondered if anyone knew she was a complete fake.

INTERMISSION

I wanted to take a moment right in the midst of the story to allow you to breathe a little. I called this chapter, "Intermission". As with any marriage, any issues that occurred didn't only affect the husband and wife, but their parents, siblings, friends, and so on. I asked my family and friends to try and recall some events that they found disturbing or emotionally challenging that maybe I didn't realize was happening. Most of my family and friends chose not to participate in recalling memories with Sara as it was too painful to relive. The following excerpt is from the few who chose to provide their memories on how they too survived Sara.

Mom:

One of the BIG things I remember about Sara and her and hateful mean behavior was the day Brian asked her to go to the go-kart races at Cedar Mills with us. Both our kids raced go-karts for years and Brian was an extremely good racer. That weekend was really hot and muggy and storms were predicated later in the evening. I just shook my head and knew that it was a big mistake, but he was really excited, so we all prepared to be on our best behavior. Dad and I bought a big white sun tent at a hardware store that morning (that we really couldn't afford at the time, but felt it would be worth it to make Sara happy) so she wouldn't have to sit in the sun and get sun burnt. Steve was racing at the time as well, and when he was around, he seemed to irritate Sara for whatever reason she could think of. I made her favorite iced tea and packed a bunch of food Brian said she liked for the day and off we went to the track.

When we got there, we set up the tent and it was pretty nice. There was plenty of room for all of us to sit in the shade. Here comes the problem. Dad and I were taking the lawn chairs out of the back of the truck, and Sara took one look and saw that there were not enough chairs for everyone and got a bitchy attitude right away. I tried to tell her that I did bring enough chairs, but she walked away and sat down on the ground in the sun, and did her pouty thing. I knew she would look like a lobster in a matter of an hour or less, but nothing I said could change her mind. I pretty much begged her to sit in a lawn chair. I offered sun screen, but that wasn't the right brand for her. Brian tried to talk to her, but nothing worked. Steve tried and they had a big argument. Steve was young and didn't take anybody's shit and saw right through her for what she was. This was before the races even started. We all had an extremely long night ahead of us, especially for Brian. The rest of the night was horrible and very tense for all of us. I thought I was going to throw up. I get sick to my stomach, and dad just gets pissed off.

The next morning was Sunday. I didn't sleep well and stewed about it all night and came to my boiling point in the morning. I was going to confront her. Dad begged me not to, but my argument was that if Brian was going to marry her, she needed to treat our family with a little respect and not be such a bitch to us. I couldn't understand what I ever did to her to make her hate me so much right away. Over the years, I began to realize that she would make up so many lies, that after a while she began to believe her own lies. They were real to her, or that's what she had people believing. At any rate, I drove over to her apartment early Sunday morning. It was about 8am. Brian had spent the night there and was walking out to his car when I drove up. He was shocked to see me and asked what I was doing there. I told him I needed to talk to Sara. He instantly knew what I meant. There was no stopping it. He followed me back into the apartment and I told Sara I needed to talk to her about last night. Things escalated extremely fast and before I knew what was happening, we were both yelling and swearing at each other. I just wanted her not to be so mean to us, and realize that last night dad and I catered to her needs for the sake of our son, because he was so excited she was finally coming to see him race. I just wanted everything nice for him, so she might show a little interest in him racing go-karts.

I remember that day very well. Brian just stood in the corner of the kitchen leaning up against the wall and slowly slid down to the floor curling his body up in a ball covering his head with his hands, crying. I know he realized that he couldn't get between me and Sara. She shook her finger at me screaming that "things are going to be different now that Brian and I are getting married" and "when Brian and I have kids, you will NEVER get to see them". She kept screaming 'she hated me' over and over and that "you and your husband never loved Brian". "No one has ever loved Brian until I came into his life". It seemed to go on for hours, but looking back, I'm sure it only lasted a few minutes. I really thought she was going to come across the kitchen table and attack me. I was scared to death. I will never forget how red and scary her face got and the look in her eyes freaked the crap out of me. I've never been that scared of anyone ever wanting to hurt me, but at that moment, I was scared of her. My heart was pounding so hard, I thought I was going to have a heart attack. I was fighting back the tears, and then she demanded me to get the hell out of her apartment right now and slammed the door behind me.

I left the apartment crying, because clearly I made my first mistake by challenging her. It felt like an out of body experience was happening to me. I have never in my life let anyone get into my head and mess with me like that. For whatever reason, instead of going home, I drove to her parent's house. This was my second mistake. I went to the front door and pounded constantly yelling for Sara's mother to open the door. I'm sure the neighbors heard me as it was a really warm Sunday and pretty quiet at that time of the morning. I kept pounding repeatedly and yelling until Sara's brother opened the door looking like he just woke up. He said his mom and dad were in church. Thinking it was a lie, I told him "you have your mother call me when she gets home about your fucking bitch sister." He looked scared, told me that he would give his mom the message and then shut the door in my face.

I drove away thinking that I needed to end this crap right now that Sara keeps pulling and being so mean to everyone. I drove straight to their church. I sat in my car for a few minutes contemplating if I dare go in the church. My plan was to find Sara's mom and dad and have it out with them right there. I took a few deep breaths to calm myself down, changed my mind and drove home. By that time it was about 10am and my Sunday was completely ruined. They had managed to destroy a perfectly beautiful Sunday.

I broke down and cried for most of that day, mostly because I knew that Sara would vent to Brian and continue to feed him lies about us. Dad was comforting to me, but gave me his "told you so" and "what did you think was going to happen" speech. That evening, Brian showed up with his long time best friend to get all his stuff and moved out. Sara fed him a bunch of lies that dad and I tossed all his stuff out on the front yard and kicked him out of our house. This was not true. That was a lie. But he was getting brainwashed by Sara, and she always gave him lots of attention and that was new for him. Dad tried to talk to Brian in the back yard up by the shed about thoughts we have had about us seeing him on a train track, and we see the train coming, but he won't get off the track. I remember watching out the bedroom window and seeing dad giving him a hug and telling him how much he loved him. Dad came in the house after Brian left, and was crying.

There were so many times during the dating and marriage years to Sara that I knew Brian was getting brainwashed, abused mentally and feeling so alone that I cried for him, so much that I swear it could fill up an ocean.

Mom & Dad:

We thought there might be a chance for our families to come together and have some kind of harmony before Sara and Brian's wedding. The day we went over to Sara's parent's house to go over the wedding plans gave me a tiny bit of hope. We all sat at the kitchen table and went over the guest list. (Mom:) "I begged dad ahead of time to be on his best behavior, keep calm and not jump to conclusions." After seeing the guest list that her parent's had prepared, it looked like they had ¾ of the grand total we all agreed on. We had about ¼ and together, Brian and Sara had a list of their own. Dad and I prepared ahead of this meeting that Sara's mom had already announced that the "bill" for the wedding will be split straight down the middle to be fair. Dad kept his mouth shut as promised, but I could tell that he was getting pissed.

Both of Sara's parents stated that their families were big beer drinkers and no hard alcohol would be provided. Sara's dad mentioned that beer was cheaper and that is the way it was going to be. Dad wanted to have a drink at the wedding, and wasn't going to drink beer. I kicked him in the leg under the table to let him know to drop it, and he did. Then Sara's dad made a comment out of the blue that it wasn't fair that we should have to pay for half of the bill when most of the people were from their family. He said that it looked like our guest list had about a fourth of the total count so we should have to pay for about a fourth of the bill instead of the half that they had previously stated. That appeared to piss Sara's mom off right away, but her dad stood his ground. I was shocked! After that, the wedding day went ok. Everyone seemed to be having fun.

Sara's mom really did a good job planning out every detail. I thought she did, and told her several times. I remember asking Brian to dance with me at his wedding, and he got really nervous and said he needed to go find Sara. I never did get that dance. I really felt bad. He seemed to avoid dad and me that night and didn't want either of us to take any pictures of him and Sara or our family together. Another night I cried.

Mom:

When Michael was born, I felt like maybe Sara had come around because she called me the night before to come to the hospital the next morning. Her surgery was scheduled around noon or so and she made me feel important that she wanted the two grandmothers with her. I got invited into her room before they took her to surgery. Brian was so excited and nervous and proud. Brian and Sara were told that Michael was going to have complications that they told us all about ahead of time so it wouldn't be so shocking after he born to see him. I remember telling Sara good luck and I loved her and then I watched them wheel her away in the bed down the hall. What seemed to be then just a matter of minutes I saw Brian coming back down the hallway with his scrubs on, wiping the tears away from his eyes. You told me and Sara's mom to come with you. I was sure that Michael didn't make it, or something bad happened. I was so scared. We were both expecting to see Michael hooked up to machines and tubes in the isolate. Much to my surprise, we saw a beautiful little baby boy wrapped in a blue blanket lying in a clear plastic hospital crib. I finally realized that he was ok and Brian was crying because he was so emotional and relieved. That is a moment I will never forget. He was so overwhelmed with joy and so proud of his new son.

After that things changed back to the abnormal for us and the normal for Sara. We couldn't just come see Michael anytime we wanted. We needed to call first and make an "appointment". Most of the time if we wanted to come over, Brian would meet us in the driveway, even in the winter, and ask us what we wanted. A lot of times we didn't even get out of the car. We felt very unwelcome. Dad and I stopped once in the winter to pick up a tool or saw or something Brian had borrowed from dad and he came running out of the house when he saw us drive up, wearing only a t-shirt and jeans and handed it to me through the car window. He told us "thanks" and ran back into the house. We drove away, I cried and dad got pissed. Most often, he wouldn't even offer us to come into their house for a lot of different reasons. He was getting really good at making up excuses and I knew every time he did. I couldn't figure out what was happening to him. I started to tear my life apart going through every moment since Brian was born over and over to try to figure out where I went wrong with him and why he treated us that way. I just didn't understand.

Mom:

Brian called me on the phone one afternoon in the fall and asked me what I was doing, and if I could come over right away and help him. I came right away, because I knew that it was my chance to see Michael. Brian had laundry going and was in a panic because Sara would be home in about an hour and the house was not cleaned up, dishes were not done and the floor was not scrubbed yet. He was almost freaking out. He just said to hurry up and scrub the floor really fast and to please load the dishwasher. I couldn't even spend a few minutes with Michael. I did what he told me to do as fast as I could and then he pretty much pushed me out the door because Sara was on her way home. I knew that things were not going well between those two. Another day I cried on my way home. I just didn't know how to help my son. I knew he were in a bad situation. Dad was getting tired of seeing me cry all the time for Brian. I really don't think a week ever went by during the time he spent with Sara that I didn't break down crying to dad about him, and knew as a mother that something bad was happening to my son, and felt completely helpless that I couldn't do something to help him. I kept having flashbacks to the day I stormed her apartment and fought with her. It didn't accomplish anything at that time, and I was sure it wouldn't help if I did that again. I really wanted to, but for Brian's sake, couldn't do that again.

Mom:

Brian did call me once in a while to talk on the phone, and I could always tell when Sara was not home because he was a completely a different person. He was really nice and would talk for a long time with me and be so calm. I really liked that and wanted you to know that I was there for him. We would have really nice talks on the phone, and sometimes in the middle of a conversation, he would abruptly tell me that you needed to go right away and hang up. I knew that he was watching out the window and saw Sara pull in the driveway. If I called him to talk, I could tell if she was home because he was really short with me and wanted to know why I was calling. He always had an excuse why he couldn't talk to me when Sara was home.

Mom:

I remember one hot afternoon that Brian was out of town with work, Dad and I came over and brought our lawn mower and cut their grass for them. Sara pulled up in the car with Michael and her mom just as we were finishing. Sara asked me what we were doing at her house while she was gone. I just told her that I love cutting grass and wanted to surprise her while Brian was away. She didn't thank us; she just said how hot it was outside and went into the house with her mom. She left us standing in the driveway. We loaded the lawnmower in the truck and came home. Dad was pissed again. I just wanted to help them out so Brian didn't have to do it when he got home that evening.

Mom:

When I heard the news that Adam was finally coming home from the country, I stopped after work at a clothing store to get him some new baby clothes. Brian told me that Adam loved the color green and frogs, so I tried to find all the green frog clothes I could. I remember calling the home phone, and Sara answered. I asked if it was ok to stop on my way home from work to drop off the presents for Adam.

She agreed. It was a beautiful sunny day, and I remember that well. When I pulled in the driveway, she met me there. She made small talk, kept looking down at the ground and gave me that fake smile and did not invite me in. I finally handed her the gift bags with the clothes I just bought, along with the gift receipts just in case she didn't like what I bought. She didn't thank me or bother to see what was inside. She said she had to get going to pick up Michael at the neighbors, so that was my queue to leave. I drove away and just cried thinking no matter how much I try to be nice to please her, she would never like me.

I called later to see if it was ok for Dad and I to come and see Adam because we hadn't seen him yet. Brian said we needed to wait until he bonded with his family first. He told us that the adoption agency said the "parents and siblings" were the only ones to be with him for about a month at first, and family members would just have to be patient and wait. Adam would be going through a lot of emotional and cultural adjustments. Some of the stories he told why we couldn't see him seemed to be "made up" in my mind because I knew that Sara's parents and family and even their family friends were at the house to see Adam right away and Sara just didn't want us there. I was so hurt and didn't understand why we were not allowed to see our new grandson, but I also understood that if I pushed the issue, Brian would "pay" for it some way somehow. We waited until he called us. We came right over. Sara seemed very crabby with us there and didn't say much. Brian made small talk with dad, and I took some pictures of Adam and remember taking a few with Michael and his new puppy, Lucy. I was so proud Brian had his little boy he fought so hard for to get home.

Several months after that I heard from other family members that Adam had had a surgical procedure done. Brian never told us, and I didn't understand why he wouldn't want us to know. I felt really bad that Adam would know we never cared enough to come see him. I went to the dairy queen and bought him a gift card for some ice cream and a get well card. I called to say I was coming over to drop it off. Brian was really nervous that afternoon. He let me come in, and kept pacing the living room floor. I figured that Sara was upstairs waiting for me to leave, so I left.

When Adam was baptized, I was so sick that day just from the stress leading up to that day. I remember coming into church with dad and my parents. Sara's family was in the front row and our family was in the second row. Sara's mom just gave me daggers when we came into church. Before church even started, I left to go to the bathroom because I thought I was going to throw up. We went over to Brian and Sara's house for cake and ice cream afterward. I remember going outside twice to throw up in the side yard. I just couldn't stand Sara and her mom sitting there, acting so nice and perfect in front of my parents and dad's parents. They didn't talk to me that day at all. I never told my mom what was going on for years. I just kept that to myself. I felt so ashamed, and I didn't want my family to know how Sara was treating Brian. If they ever found out, I was worried they would come over and say something to her and then Brian would suffer the consequences later.

Mom & Dad:

Another memory I have is the Christmas concerts at Michael's preschool. By the time Brian called us, it was usually the night before and he would always tell us that it is ok if dad and I couldn't make it on such short notice. He'd understood. The truth was he didn't call me because Sara didn't want us there. Then she could tell Michael that we didn't care to see him sing. That made perfect sense. Michael wouldn't see us there and believe her. Dad and I always came and sometimes Steven too. Brian was always super nervous with us there. But Sara's family was always there, front and center. I believed that Brian still loved us, but I felt him slipping away and becoming one of Sara's family.

We lost holidays at first. Thanksgiving was her family's favorite holiday, so Brian had to go there. Christmas Eve at our house was cut short too because Sara's family always celebrated on Christmas Eve and went to mass as a family. We switched to Christmas Day, but that was when Sara's mom made her special breakfast so Brian *needed to be there with Sara. I was losing all the holidays and there was nothing we could do about it. I prayed so hard for years for God to bring our son back to us, somehow.*

I went to morning mass on my days off work and stayed after mass for an hour or so praying the rosary all by myself and then wrote in the book intentions so the church would pray for our son too. Once and awhile a mutual family friend would come and sit with me and I would just break down and cry. She kept telling me that we raised a good son and God would answer my prayers.

To Brian:

I hope you don't hold anything against me for writing these things down, because you asked me to tell my side of the story, but ever since you met and starting dating Sara, I knew that she was not a good person. Her mom told the drumline moms one weekend when we were in the cities that Sara had always been an angry child at a very early age. She said that she and her husband would just give her anything she wanted because it was much easier than the alternative of her screaming fits until she got what she wanted. Her mom also said that she sometimes was afraid of what Sara would do if she didn't get her way. Thank you for allowing me to be a part of your story.

-Mom

Let's get back to it…

Bringing Home Our Baby

After Michael was born, we were told that we shouldn't get pregnant again due to Sara's severe complications with his birth. Sara had a bleeding disorder and when Michael was born, she bled out and they had to call in for extra units of blood. She almost didn't make it. The doctors told us the next child would not make it and most likely Sara would not make it either, so we talked about adoption. We decided to go through an agency in Minneapolis and do the Ethiopia program. Out of all the programs, Ethiopia had the quickest turn around and did not require either of us to actually go to Ethiopia. I really didn't have a solid opinion of where to adopt from. Sara was set on international. She said there was no way she was going to adopt a child stateside. She made all the choices, remember? The adoption process was grueling. It was a constant emotional rollercoaster that put tremendous strain on our already troubled marriage. One day we had great news about paperwork being approved and moving to the next stage, followed by heartbreak in finding out Ethiopia's agency overseas would be closed for three months. Up and down for two years.

There was a day where we received in the mail a large envelope. It was a child's personal information; pictures, description of who they were; their entire life in a folder. Along with this information was a letter stating that the child in the package was to be our son. There were tears shed because of the long journey we had already been on, but now it was exciting again. Our next step was for us to accept the placement and acknowledge that we agreed to have this child as our son. Once that was done, we would wait for an organization over in Ethiopia to approve it, and then basically he would come home. We did what we needed to on our end, and got word that our file was given to the organization over there and our case would be viewed in the order in which it had been received. Our agency state side here informed us that we'd most likely have information on our child's flight coming home by the end of the month. Finally, we were getting our child! Then the letter arrived.

One week before we were supposed to hear about his flight home, we got word that the organization that was to approve our adoption in Ethiopia was closing for a few months because they were moving offices.

For every rise there is a fall. Back down the rollercoaster we go. I was at work when Sara called me with this news she was reading in the letter. She was hysterical; bawling. I was trying to understand her, but all I could put together was her saying, "I quit. I don't want to do this shit anymore. I quit". I asked her what she means *she quit*, and she said, "Just that. I quit. This whole adoption, I quit." I explained how she can't quit because we have a son now! We have a picture of our son and he's coming home; she can't quit. She replied, "If you want him so bad, YOU bring him home. I'm done; seriously, I quit and I'm NOT doing this shit anymore and no one is going to make me, not even you. We've spent hundreds…thousands and for what? For nothing. For these people to fuck us around more and more. I'm done. I'm not going to throw away another penny." and she hung up. I sat there, frozen wondering what to do and looking at the picture that was sent to us that I had been keeping in my wallet. He was beautiful. This was my son and I felt that connection immediately. I felt so lost. Do I ignore my child and forever wonder what could have been and please my wife, or do I push on through without her and hopefully bring him home? One thing I knew for sure. When she said she was done, she meant it. I knew that there was no way possible I could change her mind. If I decided to continue, it would be alone; without her. Something inside me snapped and I knew what I had to do. I started driving. I drove down into St. Paul where the agency's main office was. I walked in the front door and asked to speak with the Ethiopia country specialist.

Ruth came around the corner, took us into a conference room and sat down with me while I explained what happened, she kept telling me, "It's out of anyone's control" and that we'd just "have to wait". I thanked her and asked to speak to her boss. She told me he would tell me the same thing. It's no one's fault and no one can do anything about it, it was just the nature of the procedure. I smiled, thanked her and told her if she thinks no one can truly do anything about it, she didn't know me and I'd sit right here and wait until I spoke to her boss. After about 15 minutes, a man came out and brought us back into an upstairs conference room along with four others that had been working on our case. He was a creep. He wore a suit that wasn't tailored well, with greasy slicked back hair. A man in his mid-40's, you could tell he prided himself on where he worked rather than the kind of work he did.

He continuously explained that this was the way the process worked sometimes and we'd just have to be ok with it and be patient. I became vocal and raised my voice explaining how we felt "we've been jerked around and we were supposed to have a flight and home arrival date and now we'd just have to wait?!" "I can understand your frustration" he began to say when I interrupted saying, "Bullshit. You don't understand a God damn thing. You sit here in your suit and tie and run this agency and dismiss any legitimate concern families have for what's going on with their child over in their country. I want my son! I want answers and if you cannot give me answers or my son, you are just wasting my time!" Something had come over me. I wasn't thinking; I was just speaking. He said the delay is within the American Embassy in Ethiopia. Until the Embassy provides the St Paul office with information, there's nothing anyone can do. I asked for the Embassy's contact information. He smiled, laughed a little and said, "You can't just call over to the Embassy! It doesn't work that way!" I looked at him straight faced and politely asked for the information again. He excused himself, and stepped out of the room, returning a few minutes later with a contact number. "Here ya go. You're not going to get anywhere with it though, but good luck, I guess." Without saying anything, I got up and walked out.

I began making calls over the next week during work. I called the number that was given to me. It rang into the American Embassy in Ethiopia. I probably called 20 times trying to find an actual person to talk to. Everything was automated. "Press 1 for this…press 2 for that…" Finally I heard a voice on the other end asking how they could help me. I explained my situation and asked what we could do to bring my son home. She told me it was out of her hands and that I'd have to call Immigration Services Department in Ethiopia. For the next two weeks, every day, I'd spend making calls every opportunity I had at work in between different jobs. I called Immigration Services and got transferred around to six or seven different people who basically told me I would have to deal with the Embassy. I began chasing my tail day in and day out until I got one person at the Embassy who offered to look into a few things for me.

I also decided to contact the Minnesota State Senator's office to see if they could do anything to help me out. Couldn't hurt, right? Their representative said after listening to my case that he would talk to the Senator and contact a few people to expedite things along on my behalf.

A week later, I received a call from the Senator's office explaining that they contacted the American Embassy and requested my child be brought home in expedited fashion. They explained that they'd also been in contact with the agency here in Minnesota and would coordinate the bringing home of our child. I thanked them profusely.

I tried talking to Sara about everything that was going on and who I called, and where I was at with things, and she would always interrupt me saying, "I don't care. I quit, remember? This is your deal now." All of the paperwork and documentation, fees, required personal information; I was forced to do it all by myself if I wanted my son home, so I did. I didn't ask her for anything, nor did I tell her anything else about how things were going. She wanted out, I gave it to her. Three days later, this person at the Embassy called me back and explained that there was this woman's group at the orphanage who oversaw all the international adoptions within Ethiopia and basically approved the release of the children who were in the orphanage to immigration services. They were the ones who shut down to move offices. She said that our file was on standby along with many others until the new office was up and running.

She knew our frustration and how bringing our child home kept getting pushed off, so she seemed like she was trying to help. She said it rarely happens, but if I wanted to expedite things and get our child home, it could be done if the Embassy worked along with the adoption agency stateside and country side simultaneously. It would have to be requested by the CEO of the agency and must hold a relevant issue as to why he would need to be brought home to us. She gave me the contact numbers of the CEO of the Minnesota adoption agency and who the contact person at the Ethiopian agency would be to coordinate this. In addition, she also gave me the name and number of the person in charge of expediting international adoptions at the Embassy. She told me this information was not to be released, so she was going out on a limb. I thanked her and explained that I could never repay her for what she had done to help me, and the information I received was from a phantom; I would not disclose who gave it to me. She told me there was no need for repayment. She said, "I can see you've been through enough, it's my pleasure to help you. Good luck!" I informed her that I had been in contact with the state senator and she was helping out as well. She mentioned she saw something in the case notes about that, but didn't know what it meant. Now she did.

The next day, first thing, I contacted the CEO of the adoption agency in St Paul and very politely demanded a meeting. Her secretary informed me she was booked up for two weeks with meetings and travel, but would contact me when she was available again. That wasn't good enough. Again, I left work and drove to the agency, walked in and told the lady sitting at the front desk that I was looking for the CEO of the agency. She asked if I had an appointment because her scheduled meetings were by appointment only. I mentioned that I did not, and that this matter was extremely important and I would sit on a chair and wait all day for 5 minutes with her. The lady paged someone who was on their way down. A young man wearing khakis and a tie approached me and introduced himself as the agency's CEO assistant. I thanked him for coming down here, but told him to go get his boss. He attempted to avoid the request, assuring me that he could be of assistance, so I informed him I had been in contact with the Minnesota State Senator, the American Embassy in Ethiopia as well as Immigration Services and I was advised to speak to the Minnesota agency's CEO regarding an expedite. After listening to this, he said, "ah…give me just a minute" and disappeared down a hallway.

A few minutes later, he returned and had me come with him. He brought me into a back small meeting room where this woman entered after he and I had sat down. She introduced herself giving her name, which escapes me now, and informed me that she was the CEO I had so insisted on meeting. She seemed annoyed that I was there taking up her precious time. I took a good 20 minutes explaining my situation from start to finish with her and the calls I made and the rollercoaster we'd been through. She listened and responded with, "I'm so sorry, this is not at all how the program should have worked. It seems your case fell through some major cracks. I am going to make a few calls this afternoon and see what I can do to help you bring your son home. We'll be in touch." She shook my hand and exited the room.

From this meeting to the phone call that came next, I cannot remember what length of time it was. I know it wasn't long, maybe a week if I had to guess, but Sara, Michael and I were eating dinner one night and the phone rang. It was our agency representative, Ruth. She asked me if I was sitting down. She asked me to get a pen and paper because what she had to tell me was very important. I got the items together and waited for her to explain. She said, "Delta flight (whatever number it was) from Amsterdam would be coming in April 29 to bring your son home. He will be boarding a plane from Addis Ababa, Ethiopia to Amsterdam, and then taking a connecting flight into Minneapolis/St Paul International Airport."

She went on to explain what gate, where to go, what to bring, and who could come. "Our CEO will be personally flying over to escort him home. He will be the only child coming home on that flight. Usually we bring them back in groups of 5-10, but this is a special case and it is our pleasure to do this for you." I wrote this all down with a shaking hand and tears streaming from my eyes. I thanked her over and over. She said, "There's one more thing…" "Ok," I said. "When he comes over, he will be the 100th child from the Ethiopia program that has come home, and we'd like to celebrate it. We'd like to feature your family in a news story with the Agency and feature some of the struggles you faced and hurdles you've overcome to bring him home." She told me to think about that and let her know if that's something that we'd allow. I thanked her again and hung up.

Michael kept asking what was wrong and why I was crying. I told him because his baby brother was going to be coming home finally. He began to cry and got up and hugged me, saying "Thank you Daddy". Sara was on the phone with her mom, very excited saying, "Mom, he's coming home! We did it! We finally got him to come home!" I remember thinking, "We?" I wanted so badly to stop her and tell her that she quit on me. Without the lengths I went through, he wouldn't be coming. I never got a thank you or anything. From that point on, it was "We" or "Us" that brought him home. To this day, that still bothers me.

The agency called us a day to two before we were to go to the airport to pick Adam up and asked us about the news story being that Adam would be the 100th child coming home. There was a large part of me that wanted to say, "Hell yes!" I mean, the lengths I had gone through to bring him home and now he was coming, yes. Tell our story. Before I could get my thoughts into words, Sara chimed in saying, "Absolutely not." We hadn't even talked about it really, but she had her mind made up. "So we say "yes" and then do this news story with cameras in our faces, people asking all these personal questions and then we're on the evening news with random people knocking on our door and everyone knows who we are?! Absolutely not." And then she finished her little rant by saying, "Is that what you want? All the publicity and "fame" after all we've done to bring him home?" Here we go with the "we" again. Honestly, I did want some recognition for Christ sake. I wasn't looking at getting famous in the least, but dammit, I put my job on the line, my marriage, my finances and my family to go to the lengths I had gone through to bring him home, which was never a guarantee, so yes, I wanted it, but it never mattered what I wanted. Whatever Sara said is what we did; end of story. There never was any news story. Adam came home as the 100th child, and we quietly went home.

The day we left for the airport, we stopped because Michael wanted to get Adam a balloon. He was very specific. He wanted an orange one, so we stopped and let him pick out a balloon. We arrived at the terminal and Sara sat in a chair alongside Michael. There was virtually no one there. I went up to ask the customer service booth if we were in the right area, and found that we were, it was just there weren't a lot of passengers on his flight home from Amsterdam. I kept checking the computer screen watching for status updates on his flight. I watched it change from "landing" to "unloading", then "customs". We continued to wait.

I kept pacing as I could not sit. My heart racing to see our son, the boy I fought so hard to get. He was finally here, and going to be coming through these glass doors any minute now. Sara kept telling me to come sit down but I couldn't. She sat on that bench reading a magazine. I was antsy. A few minutes later, I saw a few people trickle down the steps and through the doors. I frantically searched for someone who looked familiar and then I froze. I saw the agency's CEO come around the corner with a little boy in her arms. It was Adam. She came through the door and approached us saying, "Congratulations, here's your son." I looked at him and began to tear up, but wiped them away so I could hold him. As I began to walk up to him, Sara came out of nowhere and grabbed him saying, "I can't believe we did it. He's here! He's home! Thank you for everything you've done…" as she was talking to the staff that brought Adam home and holding him, I stood there in the background, trying to smile and not draw attention to my frustration, but I was completely baffled at what just happened. Here we go again with all the "we's". I was not given any credit for any of the struggles I faced trying to bring him home when she quit on me some 4 months ago. Michael handed Adam the balloon and smiled at him, telling him who he was and that "I'm your big brother, Adam!" There was a lot of happiness that he was home, but quite honestly, mine was mixed with frustration.

As we gathered our things, I asked Sara if I could carry him to the car and she said, "No, I've got him, you can push the stroller with the bags." Alright. We got him in the van, and began to pull away. He began to cry. We were told this may happen as children from Ethiopia were not used to vehicles. Adam had only seen donkeys or mules pulling carts, and the rare vehicle if it had come to his province from Addis. Michael attempted to console Adam, but only worked somewhat. I told Sara I could sit back there with him and she could drive home, but her response was, "No, he's fine. He'll get used to it." My heart sank, as my son continued to cry.

All of the post-adoption paperwork and fees that were required once Adam was home continued to fall on my shoulders. I would ask Sara to help me fill out the paperwork so it could get submitted back quicker, but she'd always remind me that "I quit, remember? I told you if you wanted him home, it was all you, and you continued, so...it's all you. I'm done".

And I'm not asking for value nor the pain but I am asking
For a way out of this lie

Because I can't wait for you to catch up with me
And I can't live in the past and drown myself in memories

I wonder why you make believe
You live your life straight through me
I cannot understand why you question me and then you lie
I will not justify your way's I cannot show you an escape
I do not know you any more, I never knew you anyway

The Only Way He's Gonna Learn

Adam was 13 months old when he came home from Ethiopia, and for a while, there was a transition period. For him, specifically, there were times when he would wake up from sleeping, and cry, or scream, or become somewhat hysterical. I can only imagine it was due to him not knowing where he was yet. We didn't know what actually caused it, and there were times when we were both tired and it became difficult to remain calm and patient when Michael was sleeping, and Adam was screaming. We wouldn't want him to wake his brother. Many times, I would get Adam out of his room, and take him downstairs. He was wide awake mainly due to the time difference still. It was usually between 1am and 3am. We'd sit in the rocking chair, and I'd rock him while we watched "The Fresh Prince of Bel Air" on reruns. This was our bonding time and to this day, I feel privileged to have had that time with him.

I remember times that frustration was high and Adam would wake up screaming. Sara would get angry because he wouldn't stop crying. She'd raise her voice, grab him by his arms and say, "Stop it! Stop crying! Oh, my God, child, stop it!" He would continue. It shocked me when it happened the first time. She grabbed him out of his bed and laid him on his back on the floor, still crying hysterically, and screaming. She would spread his arms out, kneel on his arms so he couldn't move and cover his mouth to silence his crying. I remember telling her to stop it because he couldn't breathe. She would snap at me and say, "He can breathe. His nose is open; I'm just covering his mouth. He needs to learn to calm the fuck down." Adam would try to break free. He would kick and squirm and use everything he had, but he didn't stand a chance against her strength. She would straddle him and do this until he stopped crying and gave up from exhaustion. At that point, she would pick him up, and lay him in bed and walk out of the room. I was furious, but would hold back my anger towards her and sadness for him, and tuck him in. I would try to whisper in his ear that I was sorry and I loved him and hoped he was ok. I could never get through what I wanted to say, because Sara would always snap at me and say, "Let's go, he's fine." I would leave Adam's bed and come with Sara because I didn't want to have to have another fight with her about this, especially in front of Michael and Adam. I regret not being more protective of him during this time. I had let him down.

This situation repeated itself multiple times over the next year or two. There were times when laying him on his back on the floor wasn't working anymore, so she'd sit cross-legged on the floor, place him between her legs and wrap her arms around him with one hand covering his mouth. He would scream, and twitch and struggle to break free of her grip, but she'd just hold him tighter. For some reason, not that any of it was ok, seeing her hold him like this was much harder to watch. I think it was watching his legs kick frantically that really bothered me. He was in a full blown panic. I would always beg her to stop and say, "Look what you're doing to our son", but she'd always glare at me and say, "This is the only way he's gonna learn who's in charge".

There was one instance when she was doing this and Adam was a bit older and stronger, and she was holding him where he managed to move her hand away from his mouth. He let out a scream and she aggressively flipped him over, spanked him hard on the butt three times. He screamed so loud, he went silent. Almost immediately, she flipped him back over like a rag doll and sat him between her legs again, and held him with her hand over his mouth again. I was crying because what I just saw scared the shit out of me. I didn't know what she was going to do, or if he was going to be ok. As soon as she had him in her grips again, I came up to her, and tried to pull her arm off of his mouth as he was kicking and squirming. I pulled her hand away and Adam let out a blood curdling scream again. Sara swung her fist at me, hitting me twice; once in the forearm and once on my wrist before yelling "Back the fuck off you fucking asshole. I am in charge and I will handle this!" I told her she had lost her mind and I wasn't going to sit here and watch this anymore.

I could tell I really pissed her off. She got up, tossed Adam onto his bed, still screaming and shaking, and got right up in my face; nose to nose, shoving me repeatedly. I cannot remember the exact words that were yelled, but I do remember a lot of yelling, feeling her saliva hit my face, watching her point her finger into my nose and repeated shoving. . . I just sat there and took it. What I do remember is a phrase that she used virtually all the time, "Deal with it, or leave." Of course she knew I wouldn't leave, so I would deal with it.

There were times, not often, but it did happen when we either had Sara's mom or sister over for whatever reason and if Adam became hysterical, Sara wouldn't care who was over. She would lay him on his back and straddle him, or sit cross legged and hold him tight, either position, holding his mouth shut until he exhausted himself. He would squirm, kick and attempt to break free of the hold, but never could and would just give up after a few minutes of exhaustion like every other time. I remember Sara's mother becoming quite stern saying to her, "Sara May, you get your hand off his mouth this minute! What are you doing?! What are you thinking, Sara? You cannot do this to a child!" Sara would just glare at her and say, "You're not his fucking parent, are you? Do NOT tell me what to do!"

They would go back and forth until usually her mother would leave the room. Mother, husband, sister, or friend, it didn't matter who you were. She had the same response for everyone; "Do not fucking tell me what to do, this is the only way he's going to learn." More often than not, when Adam would stop fighting her grasp, and give up, she would let go, and say, "See, he's fine. Just fucking relax people, God". To this day, Michael still remembers his mom doing this to his brother; and Adam remembers it also. To my knowledge, no one ever came forward and reported her to the county, but God knows I wanted to.

I'm falling apart again
And I can't find a way to make amends
And I'm looking in both directions
But it's make believe, it's all pretend

So...
Shed some light on me
And hold me up in disbelief
And shed some light on me
And tell me something that I'll believe in

It's innocence within the maze
But I have chosen the wrong way
I'm still getting over who I was
There's no sense of trust, there's no definition of love

I know now, it's not who you are
It's who you know

And I see clearly now, which way to go
I remember the way I fell from above
And I recall the way I was

Tell me something that I'll believe
Something I'll believe

Talks With Sara's Mom

Over the years, I became close with Sara's mom. She always would have an ear to listen, or advice to give. Sometimes I felt like I was constantly complaining, but realistically, things were not good 90% of the time, and I needed to vent. We would chat when things got tough and I didn't know how to handle things, and her mom would say that she knows all this and she thought Sara needed to get help, or to talk to somebody. This was something that I agreed with and once or twice tried to tell Sara, but the couple times I tried to convince her to seek help, she would explode on me, scream, threaten, insult, or degrade me saying our marital problems were because of me.

Her mom knew everything that happened between us, except for the very personal things that no one knew about except Sara and me. Those things are detailed in this book. She knew about high school, college, the fights, arguments, how often Sara would insult and degrade me, our children, the adoption, and the things she would say to me. Her mom would tell me stories about Sara growing up, how if she didn't get her way, she's stomp her feet, and throw a tantrum until they would give in. Even as we talked, both of us would worry about Sara finding out and blowing up. It didn't matter if it was her mom or me, she'd yell the same.

I remember when Sara and I were getting divorced and I went around to say my goodbye's to everyone who'd been my in-laws for the past 10-12 years, her mom made the comment, "I knew things were bad between you to for many years, and I was surprised you made it this long before leaving. I saw it coming, and I don't blame you." For me that was nice to hear. Her family wasn't overly *bad*, it was her that was unbelievable to live with for so long.

We Should Never Have Brought Him Home

There were many nights after Sara and I would put the kids to bed that she would be just pissy. She would sit in the living room with a book in her hand, or flipping through channels on the TV. So many nights I wished for us to spend some quality time together, but instead, we'd sit in silence before going to bed. After a handful of nights doing the same thing, I asked her when we were sitting in the living room why she was withdrawn. Without looking away from whatever it was she was doing, she spoke, "We should have never gotten Adam. We should never have brought him home. It's just too hard and he's too much to handle. We should have just had one child and not messed with it." My heart sank. How could she say these things about Adam? I started thinking of what she was saying. For her, she quit long ago. It was me who pushed to bring him home, so was this my fault? Somehow I saw it coming. "Why did you insist on bring him home when all the signs pointed to leaving him there?" she asked me. Was I supposed to answer? I told her, "Because he is our son, Sara. You can't just have someone say, 'here's your child' and turn your back on him."

She turned quickly and became frustrated, "Someone would have adopted him and he'd be just fine, and we would be much better off. You should have listened to me and quit too. We wouldn't be thousands of dollars in debt and we'd be happier." I tried talking to her about some of the things that Adam does that makes her upset, but she seemed to avoid my conversation. I remember being worried about things now while I was at work. Would Sara take care of him like he needed to be taken care of, or would she neglect him? Would she straddle him and go too far while I'm at work and cause permanent damage? This wasn't the first time Sara made these comments to me about Adam. It seemed like almost every night after the kids would go to bed, Sara would vent to me about Adam and how him being here is ruining Michael's childhood. Her comments became more and more ridiculous that I remember calling her mom at one point during my work day and talking to her about some of these comments that were made.

Sara's mom saw a lot of what was going on and made it known to me that she was concerned with Sara's behavior. She would tell me as we'd often have conversations that "Sara needs help. She needs to talk to someone and get some help. This has gone too far and I'm seriously worried about her, and especially that little boy you brought home." I told her mom that I tried a couple of time to suggest that Sara go talk to somebody, but she would always get extremely angry and say that *I* was the problem, not her. I can't really remember what happened with all this, but I do know that her mom never talked to her about it, she never got help, and I continued to hear about how she regretted bringing Adam home.

The Breezeway

When we moved in to our old farm house, it had a three season breezeway connecting the house to the garage. It had shitty storm windows, only a storm door and water stained pine wood walls; somewhat cottage-looking. The first spring after we moved in, the snow started melting and our breezeway flooded. There was an inch of standing water over the entire floor. The neighbor referred to it as "The annual flood fest". At that time, I was inexperienced and uneducated with home ownership. I should've sued the previous owners for not disclosing this to us, and Sara reminded me of that virtually every day. Instead, this was our problem and had been for two years before we decided to fix it.

Sara didn't want to spend a ton of money hiring someone to fix it when I could do the work for free. I only partially agreed. I wanted someone, a professional, to do the major parts and I could help with the little things. We found Mark through word of mouth at church. Mark owned his own contracting business and did a lot of work for people that were a part of the church, along with some work on the actual church itself. Sara knew him and his family and wanted to hire him to do this project.

We had Mark over to look at everything. He advised that we completely tear the existing structure down and start from scratch. He bid the job for a solid price, and said we could make payments. The price, which escapes me, seemed reasonable so we hired him. Michael and I began spending every night ripping apart the existing breezeway. He'd wear his hardhat, vest, safety glasses and gloves and was just another worker with his dad. After the majority of the inner walls were gone, Mark brought his crew in the next day to get started. I would stop at home for lunch each day to see how things were going. Old walls were gone, new ones put up, custom roofing rafters were built to fit and connect the house and garage correctly, and so on. He seemed to be making a lot of progress until shit it the fan that one day.

I came home for lunch to check on things and Mark approached me saying the amount he bit the job for he had reached in materials alone and still needed worker's wages. He was going to have to increase the bid to finish. I looked at the accomplishment. It was a studded frame. They were just putting on ¾" plywood for the roof as we spoke. I was shocked. I asked him, "This is all you've gotten done and you're telling me you're out of money?! That you're gonna need more?!" I told him I'd have to talk to Sara and see what she wanted to do.

I went in the house and talked to Sara. She lost it. She started yelling at me telling me (as she pointed in my face) "YOU better tell him to stop immediately. He's fired. Tell him to get his shit and get off my property now! I've had it with him!" I tried to find a happy medium so we could still have him do the structure and I could help finish it or something, but she interrupted saying, "Brian, he's fired. Go tell him now before he works more and charges us more. Oh, and I'm not fucking paying him one cent more than what we agreed to, and you can tell him that." I went back outside and talked to Mark. I told him to stop and I'd finish it. He was in disbelief. I told him Sara said we weren't paying any more than what we had originally agreed to. He said, "I can understand that, but I've already went over $400 with these supplies and they're open; I can't return them." I told him again, he'd have to eat that cost because we agreed to a certain amount and that's what we'd pay. We went back and forth until Sara came out and glared at him right in the eye while she shouted, "Do you want to get paid at all? I'm about ready to kick your ass out of my property and pay you nothing. If you want anything, you'll get your shit and get out." She then looked at me and said, "I guess I have to do everything around here because you can't do a fucking thing right." And she stormed back in the house.

In the next weeks to come, I spent every free moment I had after work working on the breezeway. It was late fall, so it was getting darker quicker and cooling off at night. I would take endless trips to the hardware store across town for supplies and would hear from her every 15 minutes asking why it was taking so long, and when I'd be home. I would just shake my head. I would work on finishing framing the structure, roofing, tar papering and adding ice/water barrier to everything all by myself.

Sara would have her family over or friends to hang out with while I was working on the house. Long after dark, I'd have my halogen light out there so I could see what I was doing. Installing new windows, doors, sealing everything up with caulking or moisture barrier tape; whatever was required to pass inspection is what I spent my time doing every night; late into the night. I had a family friend stop by to do the soffit and fascia for me, but even shingling the roof I learned on the go. Our neighbor kid came over to bullshit with me for a bit and left before coming back with a coil nail gun for roofing to let me use. What a lifesaver. That made things go so much quicker. Just when I wanted so badly to be done, Sara reminded me that the inside needed to be finished before winter, and that "It's only framed ya know."

I learned how to run electrical wiring, with the help of an electrician friend of mine, wire up recessed lighting, outlets and breakers. I sheet rocked, taped and mudded. Sara called in a family friend to spray the ceiling texture and I stained, varnished and did all the base trim and crown molding. It took me a very long time and a lot of extremely late nights with little sleep to finish, but at least my wife was happy, right?

The Breezeway: The Second Round

Sara and I got into it again over the breezeway project. The same time I was insulating the exterior of the house, I was working on the breezeway. We hadn't installed the subflooring yet, so it was joisted and I had laid pink 2" foam insulation between. I had insulated and sheetrocked, and my job after work was to go to the hardware store to get more roller covers, brushes, etc; so I did. Sara was going to be painting tonight while I worked on the outside of the house again. She had come home crabby and began yelling at me about what I *should've* gotten done before she came home. I had a rough day at work and just didn't have the energy to fight with her again, so I got angry and quit for the night. She began priming the porch. I could hear her swearing under her breath from inside the house until under her breath became much louder until she was yelling the vulgarities. She called out to me to have me come to her. I approached the doorway to see her standing there with paint everywhere. She had thrown the paint roller across the room, bouncing off the corner and onto the door.

I asked her why she threw another roller across the room, and she replied, "If you wouldn't have bought shitty cheap-ass roller covers, maybe they wouldn't have been pieces of shit the get fuzz all over the wall. How am I supposed to get all this shit out? Oh, wait, *YOU* will be doing it because I fucking quit" and she walked into the house, hitting me with her shoulder as she passed. I stood there looking at the room. Like déjà vu, I got a rag and cleaner and began cleaning the paint off the door. Sara was yelling at me from the other room, and I couldn't hear what she was saying. I could hear her voice, but couldn't comprehend anything. I yelled back asking her to repeat herself, or come in to talk to me. All I heard was, "Just fucking forget it, Jesus Christ! I'm going to bed. DO NOT fucking wake me up when you come."

Siding The House

Sara and I bought our home in the winter of 2003, if I remember correctly. It was a 120 year old farm house that had some character, but after finding out that I could really do anything, build anything, and fix anything, Sara developed a "to do" list. What I knew how to do, I did, and what I didn't know, you can bet your ass I learned quick. We moved in, got settled, and waited a short time before having Michael. There were many home projects we either remodeled or renovated. I'm not sure there was any part of the house we left alone, EVERYTHING got a makeover. One of the other major projects I remember was residing the house.

The current siding was a slate siding with asbestos in it and was broken in many areas, missing paint and otherwise just falling apart. I was working at a high paying by now, so money was quite honestly not an issue. We had roughly $12,000 in the bank, give or take at any given moment. Whatever she wanted, she got; no questions. We went to the local hardware store and priced out new hardboard siding. There was a slight disagreement in that because I felt that if we were tearing off all this siding that we should just put up maintenance free siding, but I quickly lost that argument as I did most of them. We had our plan and I began tearing off the old siding after work, into the evening and on weekends. I really didn't have time for anything else. Sure, her dad helped here and there, but ultimately it was my project. I tore off all the siding, patched or replaced any rotted or missing exterior walls and installed vapor barrier insulating foam. Everything was taped and sealed according to the building inspector's guidelines. The building inspector was one hell of a guy. After I had to fire Mark with the breezeway issue, it became known to the city that I was basically rebuilding this house on my own, and rumors were spreading about the kind of person Sara was, so the building inspector helped me by explaining what was expected to pass inspection. Everything I did, he came, checked and signed off on it.

I brought the siding home and set up my sawhorses in the back yard and with all my tools scattered in the area, and began the residing. The siding was 8"x 12' and heavy as hell. Each piece was manageable, but for every piece I lifted, they began to feel heavier and heavier as I went until I could barely lift another piece. My arms were dead. In addition to struggling with the weight of the pieces after lifting many of them, they would bend and wobble and become difficult to handle all by myself. When I could, I'd ask her dad for help, and he would if he could, but a lot of the time, he was working, or was at home and didn't want to come out at that moment. I remember going in the house and talking to Sara about how heavy this siding was and the hard time I was having trying to get it up to the house, hold it, hammer it and make sure it was straight. I said I couldn't do it all by myself. Usually by the time I started, it was dinner time. She would reply to my concerns with, "Well, it needs to get done, so I'm not sure what to tell you." I asked her, "Can't I just let it sit until I get some help?" "No, it needs to be put up. I'm not going to have a house sitting here looking like shit with everything torn off of it. You'll have to just figure something out." I was so frustrated. I went outside and tried to figure out a way to do this all by myself. I would start the nail one inch down in three places; on each end and one in the middle. Then I would carry it up to the house and nail one end with the other on the ground. I'd walk to the other side and nail that up, checking the level and then finish with the middle. It seemed to work alright, but took much longer than Sara wanted it to take.

She would come out at various times to see how it was going and comment saying, "That's all you've gotten done? What in the hell have you been doing?!" I remember just glaring at her when she'd do this and ignore her. Once I was about 4-5 layers up from the bottom, I needed to start using a ladder because I just couldn't reach where I needed to nail the siding. Again, no one to help and now it had been getting dark. I came in the house and told her I was going to have to be done for the night. She looked at me, "Ah, no you're not. Is that side of the house done?" I'd say, "No, it's 4-5 pieces high and I just can't reach anymore. I need help, plus it's getting dark; it's getting hard to see." "Well, you have that light thing, don't you? Use that and keep going." My halogen light? Because that's a great idea. She was sitting in the recliner watching TV this entire time I was outside. Part of me wanted to ask her to come help me, but I knew for damn sure I didn't want her anywhere near me out there. I had enough to worry about without her adding to it. Exhausted and burnt out, I headed to the garage to get my halogen light. I ran the extension cord out to the lawn and plugged it in. Make shift daylight once again. Back to work.

I can't remember how late it was, but it was dark and the temp had dropped. I remember one of the nights I was installing this siding, I was working well past 1:00am. I would do the same as I'd done before. Starting three nails in the hardboard siding, then I'd balance it in the middle, slowly walk up the ladder and try to get that center nail to bite into the side of the house before I dropped the piece of siding. I remember being so frustrated that it brought me to tears. I wanted to badly to give up; to quit and start again tomorrow, but that was not an option. My arms were in such pain, fingers and knuckles bleeding, but I continued.

Siding after siding, walking it up the side of the house, I continued. Sara was still inside flipping through channels. God, I was so pissed at her. I'd come down the ladder and laid another piece up on the sawhorses, when I was measuring it out one night around 9:30pm or 10:00pm, I was making cuts to fit around windows and the neighbor guy, Ed came out. "Hey" he said, as I walked across my yard to talk to him, leaning on the fence. "Ya need a little help there? I've been watching you for the past couple days and it looks like you could use a hand. I know this ain't easy work to do, especially alone." I maintained my emotional composure and tried to play it off as no big deal and I had it, but Ed was one of those guys who knew what was going on. He was a compassionate man and would do anything for anyone anytime. I thanked him and said that I better just work at it, and made the comment, "Ya gotta keep going to keep the wife happy, ya know?" He smiled a little and said, "I'll tell ya what. The boys and I will stop over tomorrow morning to help you out. No argument, ok?" Giving up, I said, "ok, thanks Ed." "Don't mention it, I feel for ya, I really do. We'll see ya tomorrow."

I walked back to the work area and looked at what I had completed so far. I was ¾ of the way up the house, and everything looked fairly straight; as straight as I could make it by myself. I was happy with it and that's all that mattered; right? I heard a door close and turned to see Sara standing there asking how it was going. I told her I wanted to be done for the night as it was nearly 11:30pm by now and how Ed and the boys would be coming over tomorrow to help.

She walked out into the yard and looked up at the house. "There's A LOT of crooked pieces, hun. You're gonna fix them, right?" Ok, trick question. If I say, "no", which I wasn't planning on it, that meant another fight about how I do a shitty job at things, or if I say, "yes" that I would fix it, I really didn't want to redo everything I'd done, and that would mean tomorrow when Ed and his kids came over, they'd have to redo what I spend hours doing tonight. I decided to be honest. I said, "Well, I wasn't planning on it. It was hard enough to get it that straight all by myself. I think I'm just going to keep going. You'll hardly notice when it's all done." She stood there looking at the siding for a moment and said, "Well, I think you should fix it. No sense in doing things half assed." I replied, "That means I have to have Ed and his kids redo what I just put up." "Sure does. Clean up your stuff and come in for the night. I'm going to bed; it's late." She went in the house and I stood there staring at the hours of work I had just done, now wasted because of what she wanted.

It was Saturday morning and Ed and his two teenage boys came over with ladders, hammers and tool aprons. I explained the conversation Sara and I had the night before and what I was supposed to fix, and without letting me finish, Ed said, "Hey, I get it, we'll do what we need to do to please her and continue from there." They removed the nails and took off 3 or 4 layers of siding and leveled them better. Ed had told me, "These aren't even really that far off level." It didn't matter; I wasn't the one making the decisions. We would work at the house for the better part of the day and when the neighbors went home for the day, I would continue to work on it into the night, again; back under halogen lighting and trying to not draw attention to myself, as if that was at all possible.

I finally got all the siding on and cleaned up my tools and came in the house and just collapsed. I was exhausted. "Is all the siding up now? Are all the joints caulked? Is it ready to be painted?" I couldn't speak, so I just nodded "yes". "Ok, tomorrow we'll go to the store to get paint and start painting." I ignored her comment and went to bed. I couldn't feel most of my body, and I was completely physically exhausted, but I had a feeling my work was just beginning.

The Visa

I got home from work one day after having only arguments with Sara while I was at work to find her waiting for me. I walked in the door and she said, "We need to find Adam's Visa card. I need the information on it for some paperwork." We had kept all Adam's adoption stuff in a green Rubbermaid tote in our upstairs closet; the one she wanted to put my drums in. Everything was in that tote; his lifebook, pictures, his baby DVD, documents, his Visa; everything. I told her that it was in that tote. She looked at me and said, "If it was in there, do you think I would be asking you for your fucking help to find it?! I'm not a fucking retard."

Without saying anything I followed her upstairs into the warm, humid closet. We sat there sifting through the tote to find everything in it; including what I knew was the Visa. It was in a wallet-like slip and was stamped from Amsterdam. This was it. I held it up and said, "here it is." "No! That's not it. It's a hard-card, not a stamped picture in a book." Confused I stared at the Visa looking at each page. I *knew* this was it; but was there another? Was there a hard card? I really didn't know, so I continued to look. Sara immediately asked me, "What the hell did you do with it?!" *Me?* Why was this my fault? I told her, "I didn't do anything with it, I hadn't been in here." "Don't fucking lie to me you asshole. You fucking lost it, now he's probably going to be deported. That will be your fucking fault and your job to figure out a way to get him back. God damn it Brian!" She got up, threw the tote cover at me and walked away. I sat there, and began to cry. My heart ached so much it was hard to breathe. I tried to take a deep breath in, but it stabbed me. So many things I wanted to say to her, but I knew better.

She came stomping upstairs with a lightbulb and said, "Make yourself worthwhile and put this in the closet" as she threw the bulb at me. It hit my foot and broke, cutting my skin. By the time it broke, she was already back downstairs. It didn't hurt, but it bled; a lot. I wiped the blood and went to get a bandaid before she found out. I really didn't want to get into it with her about this too.

Kansas City: First Session

I was required to go to Kansas City for training for work. I was gone for four sessions, each session being two full weeks. They allowed full expenses while I was gone. The company paid for the hotel room, but everything else was out of pocket, then reimbursed fully. Sara knew this and had this great idea. She told me, "If you don't spend anything, you can say you spend $7.00 for breakfast, $8.00 for lunch and $15.00 for dinner"- which was the daily max I could claim for reimbursement without proving with a receipt. Anything outside of $30/day would be lost out of pocket if I didn't have a receipt proving what I paid. She said, "You could make an extra $420 easy! Do you know what we could do with an extra $420?!" In theory it sounded awesome, but realistically that would mean I couldn't eat, or spend any money at all, and we already had a huge balance in our checking account. She also found that I was given a flat rate for gas, so if I didn't go anywhere else while there, we'd profit that too. Why would I have to do this when we had over $12,000 in the bank!

In the weeks leading up to leaving for Kansas, the guys I was going to be going with were all talking about things to do and bars to go to. It was known throughout the entire company that Kansas City was a vacation, two weeks of partying and comradery. I was somewhat still a newly hired employee and wanted to fit in and didn't want to just sit in a room, not going anywhere, not eating anything. I told Sara I'd do everything to make some money while there. I had already made up my mind that I was going to cut the leash for these two weeks and enjoy myself for once. After all I would be over 535 miles away from her. What could she do?

The morning I was to leave I was packing a suitcase and loading the Saturn for the trip. I told Sara that Shinedown had their second album out and I wanted to stop and buy it for the ride there, after all, it was about an eight hour drive. They had a previous album out that I'd been asking to get for almost a year now, but never was "allowed" to get it. To this request, she said, "No, you're not spending anything that's not a necessity." I agreed reluctantly. I had everything loaded and said goodbye. She told me to call her when I got there so she knew I made it. I agreed. I started out on the interstate heading South through Iowa. After 8 hours of driving, I made it into Lenexa, Kansas where my hotel was. I checked in, found my room, and called Sara while I was on my way to a music store. I told her I was there, found my room and was going to get something to eat. She reminded me to eat super cheap so we could profit from this trip. I told her I remembered. We said goodnight and hung up as I walked into the store. I walked straight to the CD section, under the letter "S" and found Shinedown. They had both their first and second albums, so without hesitation, I grabbed them both and proceeded to the check out. I got in the car and before I even put it in drive, I unwrapped the packaging and put in the first CD. I remember hearing the opening guitar part to "Fly From The Inside" got a chill, and felt a rush of freedom wash over me. I drove around Lenexa and Overland Park listening to every song as loud as my speakers would go and relating to every word sung. It felt like they were singing to me about my life. I'd never gravitated towards music like this before. This was all new, emotional, raw, powerful and motivating. I loved it.

Here's the weight of the world on my shoulders
Here's the weight of the world on my shoulders
On my shoulders
All alone I pierce the chain
And on and on the sting remains
And dying eyes consume me now
The voice inside screams out loud

I am focused on what I am after
The key to the next open chapter
Cause I found a way to steal the sun from the sky
Long live that day that I decided to fly from the inside

Every day a new deception
Pick your scene and take direction
And on and on I search to connect
But I don't wear a mask and I have no regrets

I am focused on what I am after
The key to the next open chapter

I can't escape the pain
I can't control the rage

Sometimes I think that I'm gonna go insane
I'm not against what's right
I'm not for what's wrong
I'm just making my way and I'm gone

Here's the weight of the world on my shoulders

It was around 10:30pm and I was getting ready for bed in my room when my phone rang. It was Sara. "Hello?" I said as I answered the phone. "So, I see you're already pissing away money before you even get there, huh?" I told her I didn't know what she was talking about and she said, "So, what did you buy at some music store tonight for $22?" Oh shit. How did she know? She told me she had just checked the bank website watching my spending and saw I had spent $22 at a music store today and wanted to know what I spent it on. I told her the two Shinedown CD's I've been wanting. She laughed this pissed off laugh and said, "Well, that's fine. It just means you spent your eating money, so have fun with that." and she hung up. For some reason I didn't care. She was over 500 miles away and couldn't touch me. Even if it lasted only two weeks, I was going to enjoy my freedom from Sara and her nastiness. Things most likely would get really bad when I got home, but that was 12 days away. The hell with it!

I went to class each day, out to lunch each day, and ordered what I wanted. Each night, there'd be a knock on my door or a phone call asking me to go out to the bar, and sometimes I would dismiss it and study in my room, but on Monday's at this bar called "Big Mike's" was dollar drinks until close, and my two very good friends gave me shit saying, "Hey, a bar that you actually can afford!" They knew my situation with Sara and although I'm sure they felt bad for me somewhere in there, they never missed an opportunity to give me hell about it. I got showered, dressed and met them in the lobby to take a cab to Big Mike's. The place was packed. I remember there were beautiful college women from wall to wall, each one with a drink in their hand. I remember it being very loud and smoky. Jeff, one of the guys I hired with declared this night, "Get Brian drunk night". And the seven others I was with were all in agreement. Drinks kept coming until the room was a complete blur. We all lived with no regrets. I smoked cigarettes and drank whatever was in front of me, and became ten feet tall and bulletproof. My head was thumping from the bass of the PA system and I began to love everyone who talked to me.

Honesty began to spill as conversations were had about back home. From what I was told, I talked a lot of shit about Sara and how I wished I had the balls to walk away, but we had kids and I couldn't leave them. I went on and on. I had also been told that I told them I hadn't had sex in well over a year or two and it was killing me. I don't remember this, but each one of them at that table that night remembers it. The "Get Brian drunk night" quickly turned into a "Get Brian laid night". They began to dare me to do things, and I was so intoxicated, I'd do anything. Nick, the other guy I hired with leaned into me and said, "I'll tell ya what. Pick any girl here tonight and if you can get her to leave with you, we'll pay for a cab and make sure you two get to your room so you can get laid." I remember hearing this and looked around a completely blurry room and found a brunette in the far side of the bar looking towards me. I got off my stool, stumbled a little, but both Nick and Jeff grabbed me and got me upright. I found my focus and walked up to this early 20 something woman. I remember looking at her and saying, "I think you're beautiful and would like to buy you a drink and take you to my hotel room." The only thing I can guarantee is it did not come out like that. I'm sure it involved more slurring and spitting, and was not nearly as suave as I had intended it to be. I remember her laughing at me and her friends calling me a fucking nerd. Humiliated, I turned and walked back to the table to see the group of guys laughing their assess off. I grabbed my coat and walked out the door to leave.

They raced after me, hailed a cab and rode back to the hotel with me. I remember laying across the back seat of the cab and Jeff talking to Nick trying to see what else they could have me do, but Nick saying, "Naw, we're gonna get him back to bed. He's done". I remember falling asleep in the cab and Nick and Jeff lifting me and putting my arm around each of them while they dragged my lifeless body through the lobby into the elevator. When we got to my floor, they drug me to my room, Nick grabbed my room key from my back pocket and opened my door. I fell to the floor. The used their feet and shoved me in the door as it closed.

I awoke the next morning, on the floor, naked, and saw a dozen empty water bottles all around me. My head was pounding and I had no clue how I got back to my room, or why I was naked. I grabbed my phone to see six missed calls and three voicemails from Sara screaming at me asking me where the fuck I was. I called her back praying she wasn't still pissed. She said I worried her because she tried to call me last night and I never answered. I told her I went out with the guys. "…And how much fucking money did you piss away this time?" she interrupted. She asked me if I was drunk because she could hear it in my voice. I denied it. She asked me if I did anything stupid. I denied that too. Then she said, "I know you're fucking lying to me and we'll talk about that later, but for now I have to go to work." And she hung up.

I lie here alone and wonder why
That I come alive, just before I have to hide.

Because I believe I'm losing my nerve
But could I ever do better than this

Because all I ever wanted was a place to call my home
To shelter me when I am there and to miss me when I'm gone
All I ever wanted was a place to call my own
Where stars will dance and sun still shines and the storms feel free to roam

I listen if only for a while
But I can't decide if I'm aware that I'm on trial

If there's a way to a remedy then lead me straight to it
If there's a path or a door I missed , then show me now, show me this

I think I must have listened to that song a million times while sitting alone in my room in that Kansas hotel. That afternoon when school was done, I looked up tattoo parlors in the phone book. I'd wanted another tattoo for months and Sara kept telling me "when we get a little more money." How much more than $12,000 did she want?! The fact was, she didn't want me getting tattoos. I had one already; my first. It was just Michael's name on my shoulder. That was my gateway. I found a place that did tattoos that wasn't too far from me. I called up Nick and we went. I went in, showed the guy behind the counter what I wanted and set up an appointment. The next day I went in after school again and sat down to have a tattoo of a leaf put on my left bicep. It was the leaf of a

Maple tree that Michael and I planted back home. It was also symbolic of change. Always changing, always coming back to have new life after dying.

I was so excited about getting this tattoo that I had him schedule another in two days. In two days I went back and had an eagles head put on my back left shoulder. Nick pulled me aside that night and talked to me. He said, "Look, man, I know you're in this whole 'live it up while you can' phase, but seriously, you're gonna have to go home and face Sara, now with these two big tattoos and everything else that's going on. She's gonna kill you." I told her I didn't care. Of course 500 some miles way, I was bulletproof, but that all ended way too soon.

On a Friday afternoon, I was back home as I pulled into the driveway and brought my things in the house. My heart was racing and I was so nervous I was sick to my stomach. Sara seemed excited to see me, so I thought this was the best time to spill the beans. I blurted out, "I got a tattoo…" Her face dropped and she became angry. "Where." She said and I rolled up my sleeve to show her the leaf. "Are you fucking kidding me, Brian??! How much was that?!?" I told her it was $80 because I had him do two and he gave me a discount." "TWO???" She pulled up my shirt seeing the eagle. "You're a piece of shit, you know that?" she said as she dropped my shirt and walked into the other room. Welcome home, back to reality.

I caught a chill
and it's still frozen on my skin
I think about why
I'm alone, by myself
No one else to explain
how far do I go?
No one knows
If the end is so much better, why don't we just live forever?
Don't tell me I'm the last one in line
Don't tell me I'm too late this time

I don't want to live
To waste another day

Underneath the shadow of mistakes I made
Cause I feel like I'm breaking inside
I don't want to fall and say I lost it all
'Cause baby there's a part of me to hit the wall
Leaving pieces of me behind
And I feel like I'm breaking inside

Out here, nothings clear
Except the moment I decided to move on and I ignited
Disappear into the fear
You know there ain't no comin' back
When you're still carrying the past
You can't erase, separate
Cigarette in my hand,
Hope you all understand

I won't be the last one in line
I finally figured out what's mine

Decorating the Christmas Tree

Every year, we'd go cut down our Christmas tree and let it sit for a day or so, warming up so the branches would drop and we could decorate it. She said she loved Christmas and stringing the lights was her favorite part. She was not one to get a thick, full tree. She liked the ones that were open and whose branches were sporadic. Personally, I was indifferent. The ones that were more open were more difficult to decorate because you could see the gaps. Every year, she'd string the lights top to bottom, run the beaded garland and turn the lights on to see how even they were. More often than not, they needed some work; adjusting or in some cases to be completely re-strung. If it wasn't absolutely perfect the first time, she got pissed, started swearing about how she just spent all this fucking time doing something that looks like complete shit. If I didn't offer to redo them myself for her before she snapped, she would start ripping the light strings off the tree, and pine needles would spray everywhere, and that became an even bigger problem. I would take all the garland and lights off, and carefully and strategically place the string so that it would be perfect; wrapping them around each protruding branch so when lit, it looked like a complete lighted tree. I would then run the garland to look as close to perfect as I could.

This could go one of two ways. Either I got it right the first time and she'd be pissed and say, "You seem to think you can always do everything better than me" and stomp away for a while, OR, I didn't get it exactly how she wanted it, and she get pissed, call me obscene names, insult me and demand I fix it right or to just "throw the fucking tree away". This decorating the Christmas tree fiasco would happen every single year. Every year.

Kansas City: Second Session

Because I had done this before, this trip was a little easier. As with the first trip down here, I stopped at that same Best Buy and got myself a Billy Squire CD and a Kansas CD that I wanted for my already growing collection. I still fell back on my Shinedown CD's from the first session because similar to this session, Sara and I argued and fought over the phone almost every time we talked. Like the first session, the guys and I would hit up Big Mike's again, but this time I stayed at my table. I drank until I was losing my composure again and ended up stumbling back to the hotel alone after receiving a call from Sara. I was supposed to call her when I got there and completely forgot, and she ended up calling me while we were at the bar. In front of all my guy friends, she asked me where I was and I told her. She got angry because here I was spending more money and not banking it for a profit.

When she called I was already drunk and decided to tell her to quit nagging me and leave me alone for once. I remember her yelling back, "Well, enjoy your night out, maybe you can bring some little slut back to your room to fuck so you aren't such an asshole the next time I talk to you IF I talk to you again, 'cause God knows you seem to think all you need is sex all the fucking time!" I yelled back at her, "Maybe I will, Jesus, Sara, calm the fu.." click; she hung up on me. I sat there and almost had an immediate sense of sobriety come over me. I looked around to see the guys at my table staring at me. I got up and left.

The next morning Nick met me at a McDonald's across the street from the hotel for breakfast. I was in a minor panic because I could not read the menu. It was all blurry. I wasn't drunk anymore, nor did I feel hung over. I felt fine, but had restricted vision. I had no peripheral vision and even Nick looked blurry standing right next to me. I was beginning to get scared. I had no idea what was going on; this had never happened to me before. He told me it was most likely because of stress. We talked and he let me know that he knew what was going on with Sara and said he'd be there if I ever needed to talk. I thanked him. This sucked. I spent the next two weeks depressed. Every time I called Sara to try to make amends, she'd just chew my ass for calling. Telling me that I'm wasting her time or how I was interrupting whatever it was that she was doing. Every call ended with me being pissed off with her yelling at me.

When I got home this time, she surprised me by showing me that she had the bathroom renovated. She explained that's why she was nasty to me on the phone, because every time I'd call, there were worker people over and she didn't want me to know. I'm sure there were other ways to keep that secret from me other than treating me like a burden, but that was Sara. Doing things her own way and if I didn't like it, I was invited to leave. The third and fourth session at Kansas City I don't really remember. Either nothing really happened, or I've blocked it out.

…Excuse the wall, I put it up from time to time
A silver shade, and the design is all mine
It's just a maze that everyday I seem to be stuck in
It never seems to fade away but I pray for the day it ends

I am not perfect and I don't claim to be
And if that's what you wanted
Well then I'm so sorry…

The Letter

Somewhere within the midst of our daily chaos, Sara and I had gotten Adam baptized. I can honestly say I only have some bits and pieces of this memory as I have blocked most of it out, but what I do remember is that it was Sara's day. Everything had to be done *her* way or by God you would hear about it. The actual ceremony I do not remember enough to share here, however I do remember parts of the gathering afterwards. At the time, I didn't notice what was going on, but looking back and listening to the memories of my parents, I almost wonder why anybody didn't just slap some sense into me, but then again; I'm sure they tried. I did know at the gathering, which was at our home, my mom spent some time crying outside in a secluded area because Sara had been extremely rude to her making snide comments about our family. My dad found himself outside smoking because that was the only place where sanctuary lied. During this, I do remember Sara approaching me asking why my parents were being pricks and antisocial. She said they were drawing attention to themselves. At that moment, I was very frustrated because I believed her. I noticed my dad outside and my mom had disappeared and I was pissed. *How could they just ditch out and seclude themselves?* I took it personally thinking it was because Adam wasn't biological. I had many thoughts as to why they weren't a part of the gathering, but not one of those thoughts was the truth. Even Steven had slipped his "congratulations" card in with my parent's card so that we'd get it because he didn't feel welcome coming to the baptism. I learned the truth many years later.

It was a few weeks later and I had come home from work to find Sara standing in the kitchen with the most pissed off look on her face. *Now what the hell did I do?* I asked her what was wrong and she pitched this envelope at me and said, "Besides the fact that your brother is a fucking asshole?..." After a deep sigh, I picked the envelope off the floor and opened it up as she walked in the living room. Inside was a one page typed letter from Steven. It read:

Brian,
First off, there's a lot you need to hear about this and that is the reason why I'm typing this. The second reason you're getting a letter is that I do know your phone number but I really don't respect you enough right now to dial it and some of this will

upset you but you should have the opportunity to put this down and revisit it when you've cooled off. It is important for you to read all of this carefully.

A lot of things were said in heated situations and I have tried by best to apologize for what I've said and how I've said it and have been met by you and Sara completely unwilling to hand out forgiveness. I've tried my best whether you believe it or not and you still told Michael that he wasn't supposed to talk to me. I'm done apologizing to you and Sara. If you don't accept my apology, that is your deal but as far as I'm concerned, I've moved on. This letter is NOT about you OR Sara though....it's about Michael.

You sent a very clear message to me when you returned Adam's baptism card with the note saying that you couldn't accept it. I still have it, it's a fantastic reminder to me that no matter how much I'd like to get along with family, it may never happen...That's just life, right? I guess by my sarcasm you can assume that you aren't the only one upset with someone here. You have definitely thrown a few stones back my way, which brings me back on topic. No matter what happens between me, you and Sara, I am still Michael's Godfather and as I did when you asked me, I still respect that, thank you for that, and acknowledge its importance.

Because you're still family and that does come with a shred of respect, you do need to know my intentions in the upcoming months. Uncle Steve will get Michael a gift for his birthday. Assuming I'm not welcome to give it to him directly, I will do you a favor. I will drop off a wrapped gift for Michael the day of his birthday around 2-3am. I will put it on your deck and I will be on my way. If you choose to accept HIS gift, he will get something for Christmas as well and I will assume this is how I will give Michael a gift for the following years to come. If you choose not to accept his gift by sending it back or throwing it away or whatever, I will find out because you know how that kind of thing gets discovered. If that does happen, I will not be getting Michael a gift for Christmas. Instead I will open a college fund for him and will be making 2 deposits a year into the account. Once on his birthday and once on Christmas. On this 18th birthday, after years of not getting anything from his Uncle Steven, Michael will get the entire sum of money with a copy of this letter as an explanation of why he never got anything from me.

I guess it's time for you and Sara to decide how you will be handling this.

Sincerely,
Your Mother's other Son

P.S. Now that this is cleared up if you ever have the desire for us to put some differences aside and get along, my number hasn't changed either. It's funny, after losing my brother and fiancé inside of a month, I'd like to think I'm better off *without either of you but I realize that "family" is different and even if you decide against dealing with me, if you ever need anything, I'll be there. You do what Michael and Adam to get along, right?*

Shit. How did we get here? That afternoon I listened to Sara tell me everything she wanted to say about that letter and how my brother can go Fuck himself and kiss our asses and so on and so forth. On and on she went. She was angry and I was feeding right into it. I became very angry and developed a hatred for my brother. After I got that, I did not speak to him for just about exactly one year later, until someone made me....

Bathroom Remodel

There was this moment when Sara and I were getting ready for bed in the bathroom, and she looked to me and said, "What if we swapped the sink and toilet? I just think this bathroom is not set up right." Without her even needing to say anything more, I knew I would be adding this to the already long and never ending list of home projects. I think it must have been the following week when I started by tearing off the medicine cabinet mirror, and then sheetrock, trim and base molding, then the vanity, and tub surround. One thing after another, I completely emptied the bathroom. With nothing but studded walls and a toilet left standing, Sara reminded me that she wanted the sink and toilet swapped. She asked me what I thought about that. I had learned early on that "What do you think about that?" really meant "I need you to agree with me and just do it", so when she asked me what I thought about it, I said, "Yeah, that makes sense, and I began to rip out the flooring. What once was our one, usable bathroom was now nothing but floor joists, a toilet and studded walls with wiring dangling everywhere. What a mess.

We hired a plumber to come and re-route the plumbing and run new hot and cold lines for the sink and tub. Along the way of this remodel, Sara would get crabby and realize we had no bathroom now. She would have to go to her parent's house to use the bathroom, shower, or get ready for work in the morning. It became very frustrating for her how long things were taking and I remember her getting on my case about "How much longer is this going to take?" I'd tell her that I was going as fast as I could, but no matter how fast I went, I either made mistakes or wasn't going fast enough. I had never done anything like this before. This was a complete over-haul of a bathroom and at that point, this was a project that was way over my head. She wanted new plumbing, new electrical run, moving heat ductwork; I mean everything was going to be completely re-done. This was all learn-as-you-go for me. Needless to say, the toilet and sink were swapped, new tub was installed, we moved the damn door over 16" and added a 32" door rather than the previous 30". There was nothing about this project that remained the same.

We hired a flooring installer to come in and lay new tile flooring, a tile guy to tile the entire tub surround with white 2"x5" subway tiles including around the new window I put in. We had our electrician run all new electrical wiring, install recessed lighting and a new fan. Sara wanted cable run so that we could install a small TV so when she was taking a bath, she could watch TV! All we had left was to mud and tape the walls, which caused another fight.

I cannot remember how we came across this guy to do the mudding, but he came recommended from someone who said he does incredible work. Once finished, it was very nice, but along the way, Sara lost all control of what little patience she had. This guy came in, spent an hour taping all the joints and left for the day. He showed up the next day two hours late, mudded half of some joints and left for the day again. He was supposed to return the following day, but had another obligation, so he skipped a day. The day after that, he came, mudded another half of some of the room. This pattern went on for three weeks! By the end of week 1 Sara was livid. She would tell me to call him every 30 minutes and demand he return to finish. I became the middle man just like when I had to call Scott about payment for that night I got a ticket.

When the guy would come he would show up around 11am when he told us 8am, leave for lunch for an hour or more, and return until 1:00 after saying he'd work until 3. Sara would yell at me each day to tell him to come earlier, or stay later, or work through lunch; whatever the case may be and she'd expect me to talk to him about this and report back to her. I was getting frustrated because I had Sara constantly on my back about what to do, what to say, how to say it, etc, and I wanted to handle things my own way that was less abrasive, or to tell her to talk to him herself. I was also frustrated that he bid this job at $200 and said it would take a week. Now three weeks into it and he finally finished. I remember him gathering all his stuff and coming back in and said, "Ok, I ran the hours worked and supplies, so the total is $500". Sara flipped out, swearing at him, calling him every name in the book as I stood there waiting for my turn. He became angry and started yelling back saying "The bid was for the labor hours, not the supplies". We went back and forth until he threatened to take legal action if we didn't pay the $500. I told him to wait outside and I'd talk to Sara, who now threatened that we weren't paying anything.

I told Sara he did a job, so we should pay him something. She disagreed and called me a "fucking idiot" if I thought we were paying him a single cent. In my mind, he was demanding $500, or legal action, Sara was demanding not paying at all. I told her we would pay him the $200 we agreed on and that would have to be good enough. She became so angry with me and blew up, calling me a "fucking idiot" or "such a fucking asshole" etc, but I grabbed the checkbook, wrote the check for $200, and walked outside. He was standing in the driveway on his cell phone claiming he was talking to his lawyer. Whatever. I handed him the check for $200, and he laughed at me saying, "Ok, now where's the other $300?" I explained the situation and told him that was what we were paying and if he had any problem with it, to call his lawyer and take me to court. I told him what he promised, and how he came late, left early, promised us a finished bathroom in a week and it took him three, and so on. He, very angry, but grabbed the check, turned and got in his truck and drove away. I never heard from him again, and Sara didn't speak to me for three days after that. Whatever.

Wyoming/Nebraska Tours

While I was working, my team was required to work in Gillette, Wyoming for a few months, then onto Alliance and Broken Bow, Nebraska for a few months. I would go out for eight days, and return for 6, and then repeat. I did this for roughly ten months. In talking to my co-workers about what they were all bringing, they told me they were bringing a cooler full of food and beer, and roughly $100-$200 cash for whatever. We were gone from home for eight days. Sara allowed me $20. I brought a small Little Playmate cooler with a couple various items in it for food for the drive there and home and the $20. I felt completely whipped. While my team went out each night to dinner, had drinks, went to watch bands, or to the movies, or whatever there was to pass the time after hours, I sat in my motel room and flipped through the 4-6 channels we got. I would sometimes go to whatever grocery store was local there to get a loaf of bread and some sandwich meat, using the $20, and walk through a McDonald's or Subway (which were everywhere) to get Ketchup, Mustard, Mayo packets and salt and pepper packets. I'd drink water that was provided by the company, and that was that. My eight days. I lost a lot of weight during this time. Before starting these tours, I weighed somewhere around 190-200 pounds, and by the time the ten month run was over, I was down to 160 pounds.

Sara would call me every night and talk about how stressful things were back home and shared remodeling ideas she wanted to start when I get home. I'd often hint that *everyone was going to the bar tomorrow*, or *the guys want to go out to this steakhouse tonight for dinner* or whatever to try to get her to tell me to go, or use my check card to get more cash at the ATM. I'd remind her how we had thousands in the checking account, but every time I'd bring it up, she'd say, "You're there to work, not vacation. Aren't you tired? Why not just go to sleep? Then you won't be spending any money, and you'll get the rest you need for another day's work." Defeated, I'd just agree and say goodnight, then turn my lights out, even if it meant it was 8:00pm.

There was this one tour out in Broken Bow, Nebraska, where next to the motel was a bar, and they were having a live rock band. My co-workers told me they were good and I should come over. I explained how I couldn't because I only had $20. He told me they'd take care of me, and to just come, you know "live a little". I did. The waitress asked what I wanted and I didn't want to look stupid, so I laid the $20 on the table and said, "a round." I figured that would be a good way to make some friends with these other guys that'd I'd been antisocial with, and then they'd return the favor and I'd get a few drinks for free. I mean, 4-5 guys there, not bad. After that round and a few more others, I got drunk and ended up having the other guys I was with escort me out because I was trying to get up on stage and play with the band. They said I had my fist in the air, singing to every song, spraying my beer everywhere and people were getting pissed. We left and I realized once I got in my room, that I had a bunch of missed calls and nasty voicemails on my phone that I left in the room.

I called Sara back and got quite the ass chewing. She figured I'd be in my room sleeping, and would hear my phone ring and answer. She asked me why I was slurring my words and if I'd been drinking. One thing led to another and I came clean. I told her I'd been out with the guys at the bar watching a great band. I could almost hear her glare at me through the phone. I told her she needed to let me be an adult and have at least a little fun while I was stuck in the middle of nowhere. "I'm glad you enjoyed yourself and pissed away the $20 emergency money. I'll remember that for next time" (click) she hung up. I tried calling back, but got her voicemail. I tried again; four times, voicemail all four times. I gave up and went to bed. Fuck it.

You Eat Like a Cow

Towards what ended up being the last year or so of our marriage, Sara found another annoying trait in me; my eating. For the past 28 years or so I had been feeding myself, but apparently, according to her, I had been doing it all wrong. We would be eating dinner, and no matter what it was that we were eating, Sara would criticize the way I ate. She would tell me that I ate like a fucking cow. "We're not back woods hicks, don't eat like one" she would say. If we were eating something like burgers, I was taking too big of bites. If we were eating soup, I would slurp too much. If it were salad, I was crunching too loud. Name a food, I will tell you how I ate it wrong. She told me she'd been annoyed with this for as long as she can remember, and just couldn't take it anymore.

I began finding ways to avoid eating with her. I will never forget one night at dinner time where we were eating Lasagna. I sat down and cut a piece off to eat and before I could get it to my mouth, I heard, "Ah, that's way too big of a bite. Cut it in half." I froze and tried to realize what just happened. Feeling like a two year old, I cut it in half and put it in my mouth and began to chew. I went for the other half I just cut, and again, "Why don't you wait until you're done chewing and swallow before taking another bite. You always eat too fast." By this point, I felt a rush of heat wash over me. I was pissed. I was 28 years old, and I knew how to eat. Every single meal was this way with her. Watching me eat, giving me directions and "pointers" along the way. She'd tell me, "Here's how you should eat correctly" and she would show me by taking a smaller than normal bite, putting her utensil down with her hands on her lap as she sat straight in her chair and chewed slowly. She said I should be chewing every second; "here, watch the clock…" She chewed, and chewed, and chewed. She swallowed, then grabbed her utensil and repeated the process. In my head I was thinking, "Are you fucking serious? Who eats like that?" She was insistent. Feeling completely ignorant, I replicated her way of eating just to try to get through the meal. I would chew, watching the second hand on the clock. I was angry. I was hungry, but didn't even want to eat anymore. This was bullshit. "See, now aren't you enjoying your meal more? You're actually *tasting* your food, rather than just feeding your face like a cow." "Yes," I said, but I wasn't enjoying it, not in the least. At this rate I'd have to sit here and hear her coach me for the next three hours! Whenever she'd turn to tend to Adam or Michael if they needed something cut, or help eating, I'd inhale a large bite, almost swallowing it whole just to get through the meal quicker.

Pizza was always frustrating, especially in social settings. If we were with her family, or friends or whatever, I had to abide by the same eating 'rules'. Take a bite the size of a silver dollar, chew it until it was virtually disintegrated, then swallow; pause-to 'enjoy the food', and repeat. I must have looked like a fool, but it was either that or risking causing a scene in front of whomever we were with, wherever we happened to be. Sara didn't care. If we were at Pizza Hut and I ate any way other than the way she preferred, she'd say something to me, regardless of who was within earshot of us. I had lived with enough embarrassment and humiliation with her, so I tried to avoid any more at all costs.

She hated going to any family functions of mine simply because of this issue. There were other reasons that she had, but the way my family ate was a big one for her. She said when we were all eating together, it sounded like a herd of cattle chomping their food. She compared it to "nails on a chalkboard". In all honestly, there isn't and never was anything wrong with the way I or my family ate food, it just so happened, it was just another thing she couldn't stand about me.

Grass Fed / Cage Free

Somewhere along the way, Sara became obsessed with animal rights and refused to eat… well, anything that wasn't grass fed, or cage free. Personally, I am against any level of animal cruelty, but realistically, we had two young kids and she refused to eat or even go to McDonald's, Subway, any sit down restaurant or eat at any family gathering that did not have items on the menu that were either grass fed or cage free. If the kids wanted hot dogs, we'd go spend $8-$10 per package of five at the grocery store to get the grass fed ones. Her and I argued here and there about this as it was a tremendous expense and at times very inconvenient. After we'd talk, she'd turn her reasoning to the fact that I apparently was getting fat because I ate all the food with added hormones. I was 5'10" and 170lbs, and I was getting "fat". Again, for the sake of avoiding her blowing up about something so stupid, I ignored my opinion and conformed to her way of wanting to do things. She told me that if it wasn't grass fed or cage free, I was NOT to eat it. If I did eat it, she felt that was me outwardly not supporting her decision to make healthy choices. If there were no options where we were eating, I was to eat a salad.

First it was the way I was eating; now it was what I was eating. I was an adult, and it frustrated me to no end that I was treated like a child. Furthermore, I hated the fact that if I didn't agree with her, or didn't want to conform, I was scolded like a child. I remember a few times losing my temper and getting angry with her and asked her, "Why the hell do you constantly treat me like a child?!" She would reply, "If you wouldn't act like a child, I wouldn't treat you like one." Whatever the hell that meant.

Taupe

Sara loved to paint. Well, not so much the act of painting, but she liked to change the wall color and keep things fresh and new almost constantly. It seemed as though we'd start on one end of the house painting, and by the time we painted the entire house, she was tired of the first room, and we'd re-paint it and the process would repeat. It was never ending. I remember the time she wanted to paint our bedroom taupe.

She had a vision to have our bedroom be a taupe color on the wall with white trim and base boards. Sounds simple, but I should've known it would be anything but simple. While I was at work, she had gone to the hardware store, looked through all the taupes and picked out one to have made into a gallon. That evening, she began painting. After finishing one wall, she became agitated. I asked what was the problem and she glared at me saying, "Look at the fucking wall. What do you *think* the problem is?!" I stood there staring at the wall. It looked taupe. Was I missing something? As I stood there thinking, she handed me the can of paint and said, "This isn't right. Take it into the hardware store and see if they can add some white to it." I didn't argue. I took the can in, talked to the salesperson there, and explained the situation. They added a few shots of white, shook it up and I headed back home.

She began to paint another wall and got about halfway up and started swearing and threw the roller on the ground. It was too light. Back to the hardware store I went to see the same salesperson. I explained that it was too light, so he added a few shots of some various colors to darken it up and I headed back home. This time all she had to do was open the lid. "Nope, not even close." I spent the better part of the evening going back and forth, trying to get it right, feeling more and more humiliated each time I walked in the door, until I found the hardware store closed for the evening. Taking the doctored paint can back home and telling Sara that we were done for the night was not something I wanted to do, but I had no choice. By this time the color in the can was nowhere near taupe. I didn't know what to do, or how to fix it. When I came home, I told Sara the store was closed, she said she didn't care and was going to bed. She left the room and I stood there thinking. I knew she did care and she was frustrated, but at least this crap was over for tonight. I looked around to see various shades of taupe on the walls, floor, door, mirror; virtually everywhere. I was exhausted and decided to clean it all up tomorrow.

Getting Sick

Towards the last part of Sara and my marriage, both my parents got sick. My mom developed Bell's Palsy, a condition where she lost control of half her face. She was tremendously bothered by the way she looked and could only talk out of the unaffected side of her mouth. When I found out about it, Sara rolled her eyes and said, "She's just stressed and honestly, she does it to herself. I don't feel bad for her. She's also making it out to be a way bigger deal than it really is." She convinced me that it wasn't a big deal and that my mom was making it all up to get attention. I never went to see her.

My dad was working at his job the lumber yard and they were going through changes in management and job responsibilities, and was causing him a lot of extra stress as well. One day at work, he had a stroke. He blacked out and after he came to, he was sent to the hospital. When I found out about this, again, Sara commented to me, "You're dad's an asshole and Karma caught up to him. I highly doubt it was a *stroke*. Most likely he got light headed and passed out. It happens to people who drink like he does." Sara convinced me that this was all a ploy to get me to leave her and move back in with my parents, and that none of it really happened. I never went to see him either.

I later found out the severity of the stroke and what my mom went through with her Bell's palsy. I often wondered why the world stopped when her dad got cancer, but when something happened to my parent's, we didn't even take a minute to call them, or visit them, or even send a card. I can't answer the question as to why I didn't do anything. I think it's because I was so manipulated and trained to do whatever she wanted to do, without questioning. To this day, I regret my actions during this time period.

No Other Option

With tension constantly at an all-time high and the non-existent intimacy Sara and I shared, I began wondering what was happening to our marriage. There had been many times where we'd fight and I'd tell Sara how I was feeling in this marriage and how I needed certain elements to feel loved and needed, or simply appreciated. I told her flat out that I needed intimacy; I needed some level of human touch, even if it wasn't sex, but realistically, I needed sex. I needed that closeness that most married couples have, and we never had it. I remember when we were having this particular conversation, we were driving. I told her I felt very lost and unwanted and her response to all of this was, "This is how I am, you *knew* I was like this long before you asked me to marry you. I'm NOT going to change, and you shouldn't make me feel like I need to." I told her I understood all that and said, "We've been together now for almost 8 years have had sex like, twice! Are we ever going to have sex? Are you ever going to show any intimacy with me, or is this the way it's going to be from now on?" She barked back at me, "I do not like sex! I do not like the male penis; it's gross and it's just…ew. I have absolutely no desire to EVER have sex with you; ever! Consider yourself lucky you've had it twice. That's just not important to me, so if you need that in your life, maybe this isn't going to work. And I've told you a million times, Brian, either deal with it, or leave. That's your choice." I felt that same familiar rush of emotion consume me as my heart broke again. Man, was that hard to hear that my wife never wanted to have any intimacy or sex with her husband. I felt completely to blame. Deal with it or leave, huh? Same 'ol phrase.

It was later that night that I was sitting in my chair in the living room and had my computer on my lap. I went on to Craigslist, and under the personals section, I made a post. I posted that I was looking for a normal woman who was in a similar situation as me, and how I needed to have a woman's touch since it'd been so long. I was looking for no strings attached, just sex. I explained that I was married, but my wife just wasn't interested. I sat there and re-read the post wondering what I was doing. I was scared of what would happen next. *Would I get a response? Would I actually meet someone? Would they be creepy, or weird, or unattractive? Does it matter at this point?* I hit "post" and closed the computer. I went to work the next morning and opened up my email to find a response to my post from a woman named Julia. She replied to my post asking, "Have you tried to talk to your wife about this?" I replied back, explaining the brief version of my situation. My reply, got another reply from her, and pretty soon we were having a conversation. I found out very quickly that her situation with her husband was very similar to mine. Maybe not as emotionally or mentally destructive, but it appeared she felt some level of neglect from her husband which led her on a similar path. She seemed very normal and kind. I went home that day with a very large smile on my face, and wondered if I'd ever talk to Julia again. At that point, it didn't matter. I had met someone who I could relate to, if nothing else a friend; I wasn't alone.

This place has begun to cover me
I recall the light, but the dark smothers me
I prefer the feelings I know right now
I don't worry about feeling very proud

You don't know how it feels
To be misunderstood
To reach for the sky
I thought you never would
You don't know how it feels
To be misunderstood
To reach for the sky
I thought you never would

But I'm bleeding, and my hands are bruised
From the grip that I once had on you
And I'm open for a new way
Because there's not much more that I can fake

It's almost seeing your soul for the first time
And watching the mirror show your life in rewind
Capture the ridicule of everyone
I'm tired of trying, and they wonder why I'm gone

I can't fake it

Julia

Julia and I had been chatting online for a few days and we both decided we felt safe enough and wanted to meet each other. I knew I wanted out of the marriage with Sara and Julia and I had already exchanged a picture and with all the basic back and forth chat, I wanted to see if there was something there. She was stunningly beautiful and I had never felt this way about anyone before, including Sara; it was almost drawing me to her. We decided to meet at a restaurant in Sartell around 7:00pm for a drink. I went into the bathroom at home with my phone and called in a fake trouble call for work. I then walked in to the living room and sat down, nonchalantly and asked Sara what she wanted to do tonight. Within seconds my work phone rang. The help desk told me of a "problem in Minneapolis". The exact thing I called in; perfect. I told them I'd be an hour before I was there, and I got my boots and coat on and headed out the door; to meet Julia.

It was the evening of November 10th, 2010 and I parked and waited for Julia to arrive. I didn't know what she was driving, so every car that entered I looked for the driver to look similar to the picture she sent me. She finally pulled in. I walked over to her and met her at her van then we went inside and grabbed a booth near the back of the restaurant. I sat there, across from this absolutely gorgeous woman, and we talked about how each other's marriages weren't healthy and how we were both feeling unappreciated and pushed away. I couldn't take my eyes off her. I had never even talked to a woman as attractive as Julia before. How the hell was I able to have a drink with her?! Something was very strange though as I sat across from her listening to her talk about her marriage. This thought kept racing through my mind, *This is my wife*. I thought it was crazy, and didn't understand it in the least, but something kept telling me *she is "the one"*.

Before long, Julia was sitting next to me, her hand caressing mine. She asked me if what she was doing was ok, and without hesitation, I said, "yes." It was very strange. I could've sworn we were the only two people in that entire restaurant. Everyone faded away except her. With all the possible signs I had in my past to leave Sara, none of them were enough. I knew right at that moment, they weren't enough because I was supposed to wait for Julia. We finished our drinks and headed out the door. Just before I left for home, we both sat in Julia's van and kissed for the first time. That moment changed my life forever. I knew right then and there my marriage to Sara was over. I had such strong feelings for Julia and she did for me. It was almost like we were meant to be together, like something had brought us together. It was very much one of those things where when you know...you know, and I knew she was the one I'd been waiting for all my life, and I would *have* to see her again. I got home to find Sara sitting in the living room still. I told her I was tired and wanted to go to bed. She ignored me as I got ready and went to bed. I cannot remember when Sara actually came to bed. I laid there for a few moments recalling the evening. All of the emotional pain Sara had caused me had fallen away. I became very aware that my marriage was done and Julia, without knowing, this had somehow saved my life.

Friday Night Motel

I called up Scott and explained to him that I met this person and wanted to see her again. I shared my feelings for her and explained that I had this elaborate plan to have him call me Friday night and invite me out to watch bands with him, as he usually did. That would make sense. He told me they were going to the local beer hall to watch a band, so he said that would be perfect. I told him I'd pretend like I was going to come out, but then I'd go meet Julia. He agreed. I told him I felt kind of bad because I knew this wasn't the way things should work, but I told him I had to follow my heart. He told me, "Hey, you've been living in this hell for a very long time. You have to see what's out there, or you'll kick yourself the rest of your life. No worries here, I'll cover for ya."

It was Friday around 6pm and the phone rang. Sara answered. "It's for you, it's Scott." "Hello? Yeah…oh, yeah sure, I don't have anything going on. I'll meet ya there around 7:30. Ok…G'bye." I turned to Sara and told her, "That was Scott. They're going to the bar tonight to watch this rock band and wanted me to go, so I'm going to meet him there in an hour and a half." She looked at me as if to see if I was lying or not. I went upstairs to shower and get ready.

At 7:30 I left and drove to a gas station along Hwy 23 and met Julia there. As she parked her van next to my car, she stuck her tongue out at me and smiled as she got in the car with me and we drove to a motel. I loved how sassy she was. We spent the next couple hours lying in bed naked, holding each other and talking about how we would be leaving our spouses for each other and how we'd have to do it. We made love, laughed and enjoyed each other; never wanting the night to end. It was like something out of the movies. Her husband continued to text her and Sara called a couple times. Julia would try to respond to the texts in a way to give her more time, and I'd ignore the calls, later using the fact that the band was too loud to hear my phone. We both knew that we needed to get back home. We decided that we were seriously both going to divorce our spouses and marry each other. I trusted her, and I knew she trusted me. We didn't know how it would work, but we'd figure it out. For once I knew my life would be better. I found that I couldn't stand to be away from Julia, and she would tell me the same thing. It was truly a case of love at first sight. I dropped her off at her car and went home to find

Sara in bed sleeping. I quietly climbed in and fell asleep with a smile on my face.

"I Met Someone"

I had come home from work to find Sara making dinner for the family. Eggplant, if I remember correctly. The boys were sitting at the island, complaining about how they didn't want to eat that. Sara would scold them saying, "I don't care, this is dinner and if you don't eat it, it'll go in the garbage and you won't eat at all." I told Sara to calm down, to which she turned at yelled at me. I raised my voice to her and before I knew it, I remember Michael crying, telling us to stop it because it was scaring him. She barked at him to eat his dinner and be quiet, but he continued arguing with her saying he didn't like it and "it tastes gross". She stomped over to him, quickly grabbed him by his upper arm and pulled him off his stool, which fell to the ground. Losing his balance, he yelled, "Ouch, Mommy!" She, with her other hand, spanked him hard three times telling him to "get your ass upstairs! You're done eating for tonight." He ran up the stairs crying. Adam started crying and looked scared. I stepped in saying, "Sara! God damn it! Calm down for Christ's sake!" She walked up to me, pointed her finger in my nose and yelled, "If you don't fucking like it, fucking leave you asshole, no one's keeping you here!" She then looked to Adam saying, "What?! Why are you crying?!" He just shook his head back and forth as to say he didn't know. I remember him looking very scared.

Then Sara said, "You know what?" and she walked up to Adam, as he put his arms up to block his face, she grabbed him by the arm, pulled him off the stool and shoved him towards the stairs saying, "You can go join your brother". I reached out and grabbed her arm to try to get her to let go of him. She whipped around the hit me in the bicep and said, "Get your fucking hands off me." The same time I let go, she shoved Adam towards the stairs. He fell to the ground crying then quickly crawled up the stairs bawling. I had had it. I yelled at her saying, "Do you have any idea what you're doing to our kids?! What the hell is wrong with you?!" She came up to me, and shoved me towards the door with both hands into my chest. I told her to keep her hands off me and she shoved me again saying, "What the fuck are you gonna do about it? Huh?! Are you gonna hit me? You fucking pansy! Hit me! C'mon! Fucking hit me! DO IT!!!!" When I stood there refusing to hit her, she began laughing saying, "Yeah, that's what I thought. You're just a fucking mama's boy. Get the fuck out of my house, you fucking asshole". I grabbed my keys and left. I got in my car and texted Julia saying I needed to see her. We met at a grocery store parking lot and talked. I told her I was done. I was leaving Sara. I was going to tell her tonight. She told me that if I did, she would also, as promised, but didn't know how long it would be. She asked me how long I would wait for her. I told her forever.

Let go of the mystery
And retrace all the steps where you've been
And forget all the history
And start over again

For as you can see it's up to me
For as you can see it's all on me
I can't erase it because it's with me every day
The strangest feeling that never goes away
Now I have to face it because I can't walk away
And I'm determined to until I break

Let go of all confusion
And forget the hate in their eyes
And convince yourself it's illusion
Find a reason to survive…

I pulled in the driveway back home to see Sara's sister's car there. Apparently Adam had thrown up and Sara didn't want to deal with it, so she called her sister. When I came into the house, her sister glared at me, grabbed her things and left. As she passed me she gave a quick laugh and said "You really are an asshole, God…" and slammed the door behind her.

The kids were in bed and I could hear the shower running as I came in the house. My heart racing, I walked into the bathroom. "I'm home." I said. I got no response. My mind was racing with all these things to say next, but at the same time, I couldn't grasp onto any of them. There was a moment of silence that seemed to last for an eternity. "Did you hear me?" I quietly said. With only the shower curtain separating us, she began to dig into me. "Where the fuck did you go?" I stood there in the doorway leaning on the door frame trying to think of something to say;

anything. "Brian! Where the fuck did you go? Tell me right fucking now and do not even think about fucking lying to me."

I felt nauseous. I knew that she knew something was up. My whole body was shaking at this point because I knew what I wanted to say to her, but I just couldn't get the words to come out. I stood there, frozen. What would she do if I told her about Julia? I wasn't sure I was ready for that level of anger and unpredictable hostility. Without thinking, I blurted out, "I met someone." Silence. The shower curtain flew open and I saw the infamous glare of Sara. Her eyes burning through my skin and her teeth grinding. She squinted, "I fucking knew it! Who is she? Do I know her? What's her name?" The questions continued like rapid fire.

I felt this immediate sense of extreme calm wash over me, almost an out of body sensation. I took a deep breath and answered her questions, "You don't know her. Her name doesn't matter..." She shut off the water, and grabbed her towel scolding me, "Do not fucking look at me. You do not get to see me naked anymore. Oh, my God, Brian, I cannot fucking believe we're having this conversation right now, I cannot believe you." I sat down with my back to the wall and just let her explode. There was a moment, when almost like a movie, I sat there with a slight smile of relief on my face while I could see her lips move, and the look of pure anger on her face, but all was silent. It was serene.

It was very interesting for me to watch the next four hours unfold. Almost like clockwork, Sara went through each emotional stage in hopes to try to get me to stay or reconsider leaving her. First it began, obviously, with anger. She sat down in the bathtub and laid out her demands, "Well, the first thing you're going to do is cut off all ties with this woman. You will not contact her anymore, you will not see her anymore, is that clear?" I told her, "No, that's not going to happen. Sara, you've told me for years if I didn't like it to leave. This is me leaving". Quickly, Sara molded herself into this completely other person; more of the victim. "Brian, what have I done to deserve this?" Her eyebrows raised almost as if to fight back tears, "Tell me, how many times you have met her?" "A lot". "Have you kissed her?" "Yes". "Have you slept with her? Please God say no..." "Yes". "Please tell me you at least wore a condom". "Nope".

All of a sudden Sara found tears. She began to cry. In twelve years, I think I maybe saw her cry twice. Now, she is sitting here crying, and as insensitive as it may sound, I didn't care and I didn't feel bad in the least. For me, it felt good to hurt her for once. She told me as she sat there that she thought she was going to be sick. She climbed out of the tub, and crawled to the toilet before throwing up. She continued to repeat to me, "I can't believe you did this to me, Brian… I can't believe it, I just can't believe it." I just sat there waiting for the next wave of emotion to come.

Hours had passed and I hadn't moved from the floor. My ass was numb, but I didn't care. I felt so free, it was amazing. Sara was now sitting against the wall to my left with her head in her hands. There was a long period of silence. I think she was trying to figure out what to say. Then she softly spoke, "Do you love her?" "Yes, I do". Sara laughed. "How the fuck do you know that?! How can you even say that?! You don't know what love is. After twelve years together, you all of a sudden don't love me anymore, but love this other person? You meet this slut and all of a sudden you *love* her?! That's great, Brian." I told her, "I don't expect you to understand this, but from the moment I saw her, I fell in love. I know its love because I would do anything for her; including giving my life. She's everything you're not and I know she's the one I'm supposed to be with." "Ha! Christ, Brian. So, you're telling me you're going to throw away everything we have; everything I've done for you for twelve years for this other…woman?! Is she planning on leaving her husband for you?!" I told her that "yes, she is leaving her husband for me." "How do you know? Huh? What happens if you actually leave me, and she doesn't leave? Then what? I'm not taking your sorry ass back, and that's a promise!" I told her, "We're going to get married and spend the rest of our lives together."

Sara laughed and laughed. I can imagine how strange this must have sounded, but it was the truth. I felt it in my gut. At this point, I had no reason to lie to Sara anymore.

Another long pause. "Have you thought about our kids at all? What are you going to tell them? They're going to be crushed." I told her, I understood that, but I would figure out a way to explain it in a way that they'd understand and do whatever I had to do make it as easy as possible for them.

We sat there going back and forth for another hour until Sara offered the most outrageous thought I'd ever heard, almost like she had an epiphany, "What if you don't leave? What if we have an open marriage? You would come home to me and the kids like you do now, but could go and sleep with this other woman any time you wanted to. I wouldn't ask any details or anything. You could just say, "I'm going to see so and so" and you'd leave and come home when you're done. We could do that, right?" Shocked, I said, "No!" She asked "Why, isn't that every guy's dream? To have an open marriage?" I told her, "I do not want an open marriage. I do not want to come home to you anymore. I want to come home to her, and live my life with her and be able to go to bed at night with her. I am done, Sara. I can't do this anymore. I'm done."

She went back and forth trying to think of ideas to keep me with her, but none of it was working. She asked me as we approached the four hour mark, "If you truly want to leave this marriage, I cannot stop you. All I would ask is that you do one last thing for me; for your kids." "…ok?" "Come to marriage counseling with me. Come and honestly give it 100%. If after a few sessions of you truly trying 100% to save this marriage, you still feel you want to leave me for this other person, then leave, I won't stop you." I didn't want to do this in the least. I knew this was another one of her twisted ploys to manipulate me into doing something I didn't want to do. For the sake of argument, I told her, "Ok, I'll give it a try." She thanked me and told me she loved me. I replied, "Ok". I didn't love her anymore and wasn't going to tell her I did. The truth is, I didn't even like her anymore. We had become two strangers living together under one roof and if it weren't for the two kids we had, I would have left that night.

Now, I cannot remember how this whole night ended, but I remember going to work the next day and Sara calling in sick. She called her mother to come spend time with her and our two boys. I found out that afternoon that during the day, she told her mom and sister everything that we talked about; every detail. It wasn't really a surprise; they told each other everything anyway, so I assumed she would tell them this. For the sake of the kids, I came home from work and acted like everything was normal. Like every other night, I made dinner, fed the kids, cleaned up dinner and went to work on whatever house project was currently in need of rebuilding. I think during this time it was the bedroom turned mudroom off the back of the house. For the next week or so, Sara and I acted as if nothing was going on in front of the kids. We would put them to bed, and then almost immediately we would go our separate ways. Her to the bedroom, me to the couch. I would get up before the kids, put the blankets and pillow away so Michael wouldn't question anything. The one or two times he caught me on the couch and asked why, I would tell him I wasn't feeling well, so I came down to the couch. He bought it. Sara and I lived this way for a week, maybe two through Thanksgiving and into December. It was on a day in December 2010 that I would feel the most pain I have ever felt in my life, and there was no way to prepare for it.

I remember like yesterday
You had a dream in your eyes and a smile on your face
And I'm missing those days again, yeah I'm missing those days again
And I forgot what really got in the way
Maybe the sun that wouldn't shine should be taking the blame
Cause its raining on me again, yeah its raining on me again

Stop slowing me down, stop holding me up
Quit making a scene, enough's enough.
Let's be honest, your promise, was never meant to last
So I'm taking you on, I'm calling you out.
There's nothing left for us here now.
Let's be honest, I promise, I'm never lookin' back for my sake.
For my sake.

Tell me something that's poetic at best
Make me believe there was a time that you weren't like the rest
And I'll never ask you again, and I'll never ask you again
For all the moments and the memories
No one could ever say we never had a history
But I'm leaving that all behind
And there is nothing gonna change my mind…

"It's Because You're Gay, Isn't it?"

There was no denying it, Sara and I both knew our marriage was over, but she was still holding on. It's funny, because once she found out about Julia, she tried her damnedest to be the sweet, loving, supportive wife any man would dream of. I'd wake up to freshly brewed coffee before work, and her standing near the stove in her robe making me breakfast with a smile on her face. "Good morning honey, sleep well?" she'd say. I would always wonder how a person can treat me the way she had for so long, but then turn around and do a complete 180 and make me breakfast and be all "honey", and "sweetheart" with me. For me though, I'd met Julia, fallen for her and I knew that anything Sara would do could never get me back. Physically I was still there, living a lie until I could figure out what to do to leave. Mentally, and emotionally I was gone; long gone. Sara could be the picture perfect wife, catering to my every desire and it wouldn't matter. I had left mentally and emotionally with no plan to return. As with all our ups and downs, I gravitated towards music to be my escape and solace.

Around this time, I came across a new band, Far From Falling, based out of Minnesota and felt like their songs, like those of Shinedown, were written about me. I'd buy them on iTunes, and put them on repeat. I loved the singer's voice; so emotional and full of pain. Something I could really relate to. I don't really remember how things led up to this conversation, but it was later in the evening and we had gotten into another argument and told her I didn't know if I could do this any longer; referring to working on our crumbling marriage. I remember telling her I was so lost and didn't know what to do anymore. I was sitting on our newly purchased leather chaise couch and I was crying. I remember feeling completely numb. Her morning "love" had once again turned into the insults and anger which ultimately caused me to physically give up. I remember her sitting down next to me, and holding my hands, telling me it will be alright. She was bouncing all around with anger, to kindness, to whatever would come next. She leaned in and hugged me, calming me down and said, "It's because you're gay, isn't it? Or bi-sexual maybe?" What?! Where the hell did this come from?!

I remember sitting up, confused and asked what she was talking about. She explained how I was "confused, lost and listening to a lot of Far From Falling lately". I had to have her explain it more because I was baffled at this. She explained that she knew the lead singer was gay, and good looking and how I commented as saying I liked his voice. She said, "it took me a little bit, but I finally put all the pieces together." I told her I was not gay, not that there was anything wrong with that, it just wasn't the case, and I just liked the band and felt the songs spoke to me. She told me it was to be expected that I would be in denial, and she would support me either way. She told me, "So this is why you want a divorce and why you're *claiming* you met this other woman. The truth is, it's because you're gay and aren't sure how to leave a marriage." I remember thinking how she was trying to fuck with my mind. No, I wasn't gay, I was just sick of being abused by her, but she had convinced herself that I was gay and, according to her, is why we hadn't had sex more than four times in 12 years, why I never wanted to be intimate with her, why we never held hands, why I never made any sexual advances towards her. I had a much different reason for all that, which did not include any hint of anyone being gay. I didn't know if this was her way to lessen the blow when/if I would physically leave her, but either way, I had no idea how to respond to it.

She laid me on the couch with a blanket, because we weren't sharing the bed anymore, and kissed my forehead saying goodnight and to just sleep on it. I remember her telling me before she left the living room, "Thank you for coming to me with this, I'm happy that you felt comfortable opening up to me after all we've been through." Opening up? At this point, I truly was confused. What just happened? Somehow now I'm gay, and in denial? Whoa. She's good.

Thanksgiving

I had met Julia on November 10, 2010, and kept it to myself for all of two weeks until Sara found out. Sara tried to convince me to ignore Julia and focus on our marriage. She wanted to go to marriage counseling and therapy; whatever it took to fix what was broken with me. I agreed, but only half-heartedly. I was already gone. Needless to say, if I remember correctly, Sara had told her mother and sister. We were supposed to host Thanksgiving this year in our new kitchen, dining room….hell, our new "house". I remember inviting her family into the house with a fake smile and helping bring in their various food items. Sara's sister pulled me aside in the breezeway and asked "What the fuck are you doing?!" I told her, "I'm trying to fix things"-which I wasn't. She leaned in to hug me and whispered in my ear, "Well, you better fucking fix it, I'm serious."

Sara's mother led on like everything was perfectly fine. We all sat together and shared things we're all thankful for, and of course Sara looked to me to hear my answer, which I cannot remember what it was, but most likely something generic or made up. Quite honestly, I was thankful I met Julia. She gave me a reason to not give up, a reason to live. That was what I was thankful for. She saved my life, and she didn't even know it.

At this time, we still did not have a dishwasher, so when dinner was done, I did all the dishes by myself. I didn't want to, but I also didn't want to go schmooze with her brother and father in the living room and pretend like everything was great either. Sara would come up behind me and hug me, or from across the room, say, "Love ya babe" with a smile. I knew it was all bullshit, but I would just smile and try to not lead on to what I was really thinking about. Once her family left, I remember her laying into me telling me how I could've been more present with her family there. She said I ignored all of them and they all know something's up now. I didn't care. She could yell at me all she wanted to, it didn't matter, I was done with her. It was just a matter of time until I figure out what to do, or what I should do.

The Not So Discreet Phone Call

I had come home from work one day and it wasn't long before I had gotten called back to work. I was watching the boys while Sara was upstairs in the bedroom. She said she had to make a phone call. I walked upstairs to hear her giggling, and acting flirtatious. I approached the bedroom door, which was closed and listened for a minute. She made agreeing comments about "your dumbass wife…" and "my dumbass husband…" It didn't take a rocket scientist to figure out she was talking to a guy. I knocked on the door and heard her say to the person on the other side of the phone, "Arg. Hang on, it's my dumbass husband." "What?!" I told her I had to go into work and needed to leave. She told me she was on the phone and I'd have to wait until she was done. We argued until she told the other person, "I have to let you go, the dumbass needs me to watch his kids again so he can go do whatever the hell it is he does." She giggled again saying, "Yeah, I know…" More laughing and flirting, before hanging up. I heard her footsteps stomping towards the door, and then it swung open. I stood there looking right into hear eyes, her glaring at me and she, without saying a word, walked past me, bumping my shoulder with hers as she walked downstairs. I later found out the guy she was talking to would later become her boyfriend, also known as "victim".

Getting the Christmas Tree; the Last Time

Like every other year, we met her family at the Christmas tree farm just outside of town. By this point, everyone knew Sara and I were over; well, supposedly trying to mend our broken marriage, but I think even Sara knew it was over. There was a lot of denial from her and her family. They were hopeful things would change. We brought the boys with so they could help cut down the Christmas tree and feel helpful. I remember it was incredibly cold on this day and no one wanted to be there. Sara's sister brought her boyfriend and they were looking for their tree while Sara and I were looking for ours. I don't think it would have mattered what we cut down, we were just going through the motions. We found one, and cut it down. We had it bundled up and brought it home.

Once the tree warmed up and dropped, we began decorating it the next day. We put on Christmas music and the boys were so excited to help decorate it. Adam was a little young, so he didn't really get the whole idea, but Michael was all in. I don't think Sara and I spoke two words to each other. It was tense. After we got about half done, it was getting late and we put the boys to bed. We'd finish tomorrow. If I knew then what I know now, I would have insisted they finish the tree that night, for I would not get to see it finished...

The Late Night Call

For some reason, Sara had decided in order to try to save our marriage; she wanted us to be sleeping together again. She would initiate intimacy or sex, but I just couldn't bring myself to join in. I somehow felt like I was cheating on Julia. It was strange, but it was how I felt. On December 2nd, 2010, Sara and I put the kids to bed and she and I climbed into bed. She began her initiation to sex, which I ignored. I was lying on my back and she began sliding her hand up my leg up into my groin. I wasn't sure what to do. I wanted to leave, but found myself frozen. She began kissing me, and I kissed her back, and immediately quit. It felt very awkward to kiss her. We rarely kissed, especially in the past couple years. I pulled away, as her advances grew more obvious and sexual. I remember her hand sliding into my pants as she tried to grab my penis, and I jumped away. "What the fuck is your problem?" she shouted. "I'm trying to have sex with you; you know, my *husband*, and you're acting really strange." I told her, "I'm sorry. I don't love you anymore. I can't keep pretending like I want to fix this; I don't. I don't want to have sex with you, or kiss you, or touch you or anything else. It doesn't feel right anymore.

She pulled away, and looked at me with sadness in her eyes. "You want *her* don't you?" I couldn't answer, but we both knew that was the case. As it was, I didn't feel right about sharing a bed with her anymore, but I did to avoid conflict. I told her I just wanted to go to bed. I remember her rolling over away from me, and as her sad face turned to anger she mumbled under her breath, "Good. Having you fuck me would probably feel like you were raping me anyway." I sat up and said, "What did you say?" Without moving she said, "You fucking heard me." I rolled over, and hugged the outside of the bed, making sure no part of me touched her.

Sometime around 10:30pm or so (I can't recall the exact time) the phone rang. I was awakened by Sara tapping me on the shoulder saying, "Brian, wake up, it's your mom." Confused, I took the phone as Sara sat there, with this pissed off look on her face and arms crossed. "Hello?" I said as I tried to wake myself up. It was my mom, almost hysterical, saying that Julia was in the cities at a conference for work, and her husband came down to see her and after things got heated, she told him she was leaving him for me. My mom told me that Julia tried calling my cell phone multiple times but kept getting my voicemail, so she called Steve, who called her to have her call me. As I was listening to this, my heart was racing and Sara kept asking, "What's going on, Brian? Tell me." I asked my mom, "So, what am I supposed to do?" She said, "Julia needs you. She said she needs you to come to her if you can. She's a mess. She said to tell you she *jumped*." I told her I was on my way. I hung up the phone, and took a split second to process what just happened. This was it. She left her husband. I told my wife I wanted a divorce. Ok, now what? "What the hell is going on?!" I looked at Sara as I got out of bed. "I have to go" I blurted. Sara threw the covers off and stood up blocking the door to the bedroom. "Go where?" "Julia needs me." She gave a subtle laugh of disbelief. "You're not going anywhere. She'll be fine. Get back into bed." I was now already dressed and grabbed a change of clothes that I put into a small duffle bag. "I'm leaving, Sara. And I'm leaving right now." Sara refused to move. Annoyed, I said, "Please move, Sara. There's nothing you can do anymore." She looked at me and said very matter of fact, "If you walk out this door tonight, do not expect to return. We are done. For good. I will never spend another day with you. It's over." I smiled, and said, "That's the idea, now please move." She didn't move, but didn't fight me as I walked out the door and began my hour and a half drive to the cities to meet Julia.

Once I arrived, we held each other and I let her cry and fall apart on my shoulder. We spent the night trying to sort out what happens next, but neither of us really knew. One thing we both agreed on was we were both filing for divorce and moving on with our lives; together. I held her as we fell asleep.

December 6th, 2010

After my leaving to the cities, I returned home after work for a few days as if nothing had happened, but continued to sleep on the couch as I had in the past. Sara didn't say a word to me, nor did I to her unless it involved the kids. We had talked the night of the 5th of December, after the boys decorated the tree about how it was going to be my last night at home and tomorrow I'd talk to the kids and tell them that Sara and I were separating. I spent the evening of the 5th discreetly packing up whatever I could of my clothes into garbage bags and putting them in our closet so the kids wouldn't see them. It was emotional. I wasn't at all upset in leaving her; it was the kids that I kept thinking about.

Sara and I talked about our concerns we were having about the split. Her concern was that I would financially destroy her because she was a stay-at-home mom and I made all the money, which I told her I would not abandon her and the kids, and my concern was she would take the kids from me. She swore to me saying, "Brian, I would NEVER withhold the kids from you. You're their father and they love you. I would never do that, and I hope you know that." She made me sign a piece of paper saying I wouldn't financially destroy her and she signed saying she wouldn't withhold the kids from me. Honestly the paper was a waste of time, because after I left, she cleared out our bank account and moved the kids out without telling me. So much for honesty. We talked for a bit, mostly small talk, but I remember her asking me, "So, this is it? This is what you want?" I looked at her and said, "Yeah. It is." Somewhere in the midst of our conversation and me packing my things, she told me, "I will say this. If you do actually leave, because there is still a chance you could change your mind, if you do actually leave, I will make your life a living hell. That's a promise." I didn't respond, just kept packing. I will say, she was right. For years following my leaving her, she did make my life a living hell, but that's another story.

I came home from work on December 6th at around 4pm. I met Sara in the kitchen. The boys were playing in the living room. I asked her what was going on. She said, "It's time." Time? Time for what? She said, "I want you to tell the boys you're leaving and going to be living somewhere else and get it over with. They deserve that, and I think it needs to be done now." She had that look on her face like her saying I think really meant, you're gonna do it whether you like it or not. I really didn't want another fight, so I said ok and walked into the living room. Before I began to speak, Sara pulled me aside again and told me to discreetly get my clothes and whatever else I needed into my truck so the kids wouldn't see me carrying my stuff out. She said that wouldn't be appropriate. She kept them occupied while I took a few trips up and down the stairs with garbage bags filled with my clothes and threw them in the back of my old '84 Ford F-150. It smoked like none other and overheated, but legally the Saturn that I had been driving was in her dad's name, so I was now required to drive this piece of shit.

My eyes are open wide
And by the way,
I made it through the day
I watched the world outside
By the way,
I'm leaving out today

Tell my mother,
Tell my father
I've done the best I can
To make them realize
This is my life
I hope they understand
I'm not angry, I'm just saying...
Sometimes goodbye is a second chance

Please don't cry one tear for me
I'm not afraid
Of what I have to say
This is my one and only voice
So listen close,
It's only for today

I just saw Halley's comet
She waved
Said, "Why you always running in place?"
Even the man in the moon disappeared
Somewhere in the stratosphere

Here's my chance
This is my chance

Tell my mother,
Tell my father
I've done the best I can
To make them realize
This is my life
I hope they understand
I'm not angry, I'm just saying...
Sometimes goodbye is a second chance

This song had just come out around this time and for me, it was my sign of what I needed to do. I needed to survive. I could not fathom trying to kill myself again. What if this time I actually succeeded? There was no turning back. I had my stuff loaded up and at the moment, couldn't think of anything else I needed right then and there. The rest I could get later; or so she said. I came into the living room. Sara was sitting on the recliner to my immediate right against the wall, Adam was playing Lego's next to the TV kiddie corner to my right and Michael was digging in a box for those last Christmas ornaments right in front of me next to the couch. Our Christmas tree was off to my right in the corner all decorated, and Michael working on putting the last few pieces on. I felt like I stood there taking it all in forever, but after a few seconds, Sara spoke, "Boys, Dad has something he wants to tell you..."

I remember thinking, *Bitch. Let me do this, it's hard enough without you pushing things along.* I didn't say anything. I squatted down to their level and called their names, "Michael…Adam…I need you to listen to me for just a minute, ok?" I will never forget the extreme pain I felt saying what I said next. To this day, it is still with me. "Daddy's not going to live here anymore." Adam looked at me and continued playing with his Lego's. I don't think he really grasped the concept. Immediately, Michael dropped the ornaments and began to cry. "Why, Daddy? Why can't you live here anymore?" Seeing him cry and ask me that with that look on his face completely broke me. I held out my arms and he ran up into them, knocking me over. I hugged and held him so tight. I never wanted to let him go. "I'm so sorry, Michael, I'm so sorry." He sobbed in my arms, begging me to stay. "Please don't go, Daddy, I'm sorry. You don't have to leave, Daddy. Please, please, please stay with us, Daddy, please." I could hardly breathe. This was killing me. Of all the things Sara put me through over the past 12 years, nothing came close to the pain in my heart I felt that that moment. I sat there on the floor, broken, holding him so tight; us both crying. I kept saying, "I'm so sorry bud, I'm so sorry." Sara looked over to me and said very condescendingly, "Having second thoughts yet?" I ignored her.

I could've sat there forever holding my son, and I wanted to hold him at least until he got his composure back, but that wasn't my decision to make apparently. I sat there holding him when Sara came off the chair on to the ground with us. She pulled him away from me and held him in her lap and said, "Don't worry, honey, *Mommy* will never leave you, ever. I know baby…I know, it's ok, mommy's here, and I'm not going anywhere. I'll *never* leave you. I'll always be here for you…"

I now was sitting there by myself, tears filling my eyes. Adam still playing with his Lego's, not really understanding what was going on. I went up to hug him and he hugged me and said, "I love you, Daddy, Goodbye, Daddy." I stood up and looked around one last time while I wiped my tears away. Sara looked up to me and discreetly said, "Ok, anytime now…" I just shook my head. I was pissed. My son was bawling, begging me not to leave and she was basically telling me to hurry up. Looking back, I should've demanded I stay right there, but again, that would've caused another aggressive fight, and the kids didn't need that right now. I told Michael I loved him and Adam I loved him and told them both I would talk to them tomorrow. I said goodbye, and as I turned to walk out of the house, I heard Michael bawl even louder begging me to stay; he was hysterical and I couldn't do anything to help him. This was it. It was over.

I left the spare key on the table
Never really thought I'd be able to say
I merely visit on the weekends
I lost my whole life and a dear friend

I finally put it all together,
But nothing really lasts forever
I had to make a choice that was not mine,

I had to say goodbye for the last time…

As I walked out of the house, Sara yelled out, "Please leave your key on the counter before you go." I looked at the keys in my hand, and removed the house key. I set it on the island and walked out the door, looking back only briefly at the home I spent literally my blood, sweat, and tears remodeling. This was it, it was over. I climbed in my truck, started it up, put it in drive and pulled out of the driveway, crying. I hated seeing my kids like that. I hated knowing in order to leave her, in some sense, I had to leave them. Although I do not regret leaving her for one second, I still struggle with that memory of having to leave them to this day.

I headed out to my parents where I would live until I was able to figure something else out with Julia. As I drove away, I remember thinking, even though the last 30 minutes were so unbelievably painful, I could finally let go of the past 12 years with Sara. I was out. I was free. I could breathe. She couldn't hurt me anymore. Looking back, boy was I wrong. The story of my past with Sara didn't compare to what I faced on the long road ahead of me. It was not over, not by a long shot. This was not the end of my story; this was just beginning…

I'm on the front line
Don't worry I'll be fine
the story is just beginning
I say goodbye to my weakness
so long to the regret
and now I see the world through diamond eyes

To Be Continued…..

12 Years of Insults
&
Degrading comments

"Have fun walking home, asshole"

"How could any woman be attracted to a penis? It's gross, weird looking and has nasty shit that comes out of it. Makes me wanna vomit."

"Go, walk out the fucking door if you're going to be a little pussy."

"Get the fuck out of my house."

"Ya know what, why don't you just go into her room, whip your dick out and fuck her fucking brains out. Maybe then you'll get it out of your system and stop being such a fucking prick."

"That's your decision; now get the fuck out of my house."

"Jesus-fucking-Christ, Brian, you are such a dick"

"I am not going to fucking make out with you in front of all these people. I did kiss you. If that's not good enough, kiss someone else."

"I hope you're happy. This was your fucking fault that everyone left. You can't control your fucking parents and now look what happened. God, what a great fucking wedding day. You have no fucking backbone, do you? No; I didn't think so"

"I'm tired and not in the mood, but if you absolutely have to get off, wait until I'm sleeping, then either do whatever you want to me or just jack off, I'm going to sleep."

"worthless", "piece of shit", "fucking idiot"

"You don't have any fucking clue what you're doing, do you? I'm not going to be your guinea pig. Figure your shit out, and let me know what you know what the hell you're doing."

She laughed at me sarcastically saying, "You? Stop wanting sex? Ha! Good luck with that! You're a sex addict and can't seem to live for even a single day without either annoying me with your sexual advances or jacking off. It's disgusting."

"Get the fuck out of the bed. I'm NOT sleeping with such a fucking asshole. You can sleep on the floor or in that fucking chair"

"Well? Are you gonna get yourself hard or not, or can'cha get it up? Haha.."

"I'm not going to have that huge nasty thing sliding in and out for the next 5 minutes."

"I think your penis is not normal."

"I would love to have a healthy sex life with you, but cannot when your anatomy is messed up. Have you ever thought about having it surgically altered so it was straighter? We could have sex all the time then!"

"Fine. If you want to live with a fucked up dick, then you can enjoy jacking off a crooked dick then; it's all you"

"Jesus Christ, Brian. You really are a fucking idiot!"

"You're going to do it, or don't bother coming home."

"I told you that you either fix this or don't come home. You didn't fix it, so you better find a place to stay tonight. You're such a fucking poor excuse for a man. God I fucking hate you right now. I know I'm pissed and I really don't give a shit. Deal with it or leave!"

"Roses? Seriously? I fucking hate roses, and YOU know that!"

"I'm not kidding. Take them back and get your money back. I'm not going to waste, what? $50 on some fucking ugly ass flowers. Put your coat back on, take the flowers back to the florist and get a fucking refund."

"Fuck you, you asshole!"

"Shut the fuck up!"

"Get the fuck out of my way, asshole"

"Are you trying to rape me?!"

"Well, let's go. Wipe your tears baby boy, it's time to go in and put a smile on your face. You're not going to want to cause a scene, are you?"

"Back the fuck off you fucking asshole. I am in charge and I will handle this!"

"I guess I have to do everything around here because you can't do a fucking thing right."

"Are you fucking kidding me, Brian??! How much was that?!?"

"You're a piece of shit, you know that?"

"Well, enjoy your night out, maybe you can bring some little slut back to your room to fuck so you aren't such an asshole the next time I talk to you IF I talk to you again, 'cause God knows you seem to think all you need is sex all the fucking time!"

"I have no desire to ever have sex with you; ever."

"You're such a fucking idiot."

"God, you're a fucking asshole."

"If you don't fucking like it, fucking leave you asshole, no one's keeping you here!"

"What the fuck are you gonna do about it? Huh?! Are you gonna hit me? You fucking pansy! Hit me! C'mon!"

"You're just a fucking mama's boy. Get the fuck out of my house, you fucking asshole".

"It's because you're gay, isn't it? Or bi-sexual?"

"I cannot believe I married such a fucking loser."

And the list goes on…

Acknowledgments

It took a lot of planning and trying to dig up memories or finding old journals that had been hidden these past years to make this book a possibility. Along with it, there were people that stood by me through all the shit and disasters that helped me recall various events. In addition, there were some people that got fed up with the way I was acting, or the situation that I found myself in for 12 years that decided to turn the other way and distance themselves from me. Looking back, I do not hold them responsible for anything. Whether or not I actively sought out conflict or if it was subconsciously, I take responsibility for what happened throughout those 12 years I was with Sara, even if I was not to blame. I learned many years later I was a victim of a narcissistic sociopath.

I want to give a huge thank you to my parents for holding on to me while I slipped away. You never gave up on me, and it was your prayers that brought me home on that December day. Thank you for raising me right and providing me with certain memories I had blocked out. Thank you for feeling comfortable enough to share these lost memories even though some of them were hard to hear again. All in all, they were very necessary.

I want to thank my brother for his willingness to repair the relationship that we had once upon a time, and move past the things that tore us as far apart as two brothers could get. You're one hell of a good person and I cannot begin to tell you what this did for me, even if we're still working on it. I also want you to know that I understand your reasons for not wanting to participate in the creation of this book. Even considering it briefly, I know wasn't easy. Thank you, and it's nice having you back.

To my best friend during that time (CC), thank you for being my support when I felt I had nowhere to turn. Since we were children, you always provided an ear to listen without judgment. You have been and always will be my brother from another mother.

To Scott, thank you for being my alibi that night I met Julia. Without your understanding and support, I may have never met her and who knows what ditch I may have been lying in. In a way, you may have helped save my life.

To my former neighbor and his two boys: You know who you are and I sincerely thank you for the years of support and assistance you gave while I basically re-built my 120 year old farm house. To the boys, now men, thank you for the countless tools you loaned me and a second set of hands to make my nightmare of a job a little easier, I will never forget it, and will always be grateful for your contribution during such a shitty time.

I want to thank the bands "Shinedown" and "Far From Falling" for providing music that I gravitated to and desperately needed to get me through each part of my life with Sara. You'll never know who I am, or how you helped me and may have saved my life. Your lyrics and emotional power in your music gave me hope in hopeless situations and provided me with the strength to hang on and not let go when letting go seemed like the only option I had. Throughout this book, I shared Shinedown's song lyrics of the songs I felt were written strictly for me.

To Nick, thank you for being there for me during the stints in Kansas. I appreciate you being an ear to listen when I needed to talk. Of all the people I've called my 'friends' over the years with the job we worked, you are one of the *only* people who's kept in touch; even today.

To Julia, now my wife, my true best friend and the woman who saved my life the day you met me. I felt there was no hope for me and was ready to throw it all away, but somehow fate brought us together. As soon as I kissed your lips, I felt the explosion of fireworks and at that moment my life was saved. I had a reason to live; you. Thank you for sticking next to me even when things got nasty. You're incredibly strong, loving, supportive, compassionate, sexy, gorgeous, and funny; oh, and sassy! You are the type of woman every good man deserves to spend their life with. Thank you for being you and allowing me the pleasure of spending the rest of my life with you. It's always an adventure, always exciting, always fun, always happy. I enjoy smiling with you and cannot get enough of your company. You truly are the best thing that has ever happened to me.

To anyone who lived parallel to me during this time, or whoever may have been involved in Sara and my marriage one way or another who felt my leaving was wrong or unjust, please try to understand the corner I was backed into and the lack of options I had living with a malignant narcissist. Suicide as an option was becoming more and more on the forefront of my mind and I never knew if my unsuccessful attempts would soon catch up to me and I would, in fact, become successful. As unfortunate and frowned upon as it may be to meet a woman while still married, and leave Sara for this other woman, it truly saved my life, and for that, I do not feel selfish, nor do I regret it.

To the reader. Thank you for reading my story. I wanted to tell it so that people will know that there are relationships or marriages out there that are extremely toxic and although one of the members of the marriage may try like hell to save it, sometimes finding the courage to walk away is far nobler, and safer than staying and living with constant emotional, mental and physical abuse. This was my story, not anyone else's. Thanks for reading.

-Brian Morgan

Thank you.

Please visit my Official Facebook page entitled *"**Surviving Sara**"* and share your thoughts on the book, personal experiences with a narcissist, or ask questions you may have about the book. I will do my best to answer!

Feel free to contact me with your opinion, thoughts, feelings about the book, or leave

your questions for me regarding the book at my email address:

brianmorganofficial@gmail.com.

-Brian Morgan

Made in the USA
San Bernardino, CA
27 August 2016